2019 sixth edition

THE COMPLETE GUIDE TO

DIRECT BS/MD PROGRAMS

Full List of Programs
How to Gain Admission
Essay & Resume Prep
Advanced Interview Prep
Advice from Current Students

ROBIN KURIAKOSE M.D.

[this page intentionally left blank]

The Complete Guide to Direct BS/MD Programs

[SIXTH EDITION]

Understanding and Preparing for
Combined BS/MD Programs

Robin K. Kuriakose, M.D.
www.directBSMD.com

For the most up-to-date information, visit www.directbsmd.com

Contents

* * * * *

Preface

By creating this guide, I wanted to educate students and parents about Direct BS/MD or BA/MD programs, relatively unknown yet highly competitive educational programs across the country for students interested in a career in medicine. I also wanted to make sure that those looking into these programs would not have to spend the countless hours I spent to research what it takes to apply, how to get in, and all the available programs in the country. In the first year of this book's publication, I spent countless hours scouring the Internet, looking at several different websites until I could come up with a full list of programs. By including the programs' minimum or average requirements, it would be easy for all potential applicants to quickly narrow down which programs they would be suitable for, and linking each program's website gave users instant and detailed information about the respective program. While this information is updated yearly and available for free on the website, this book serves to add an extra dimension by giving a more detailed and expansive insight into these programs.

I was lucky enough to have discovered the existence and value of these programs from friends and family who have gone through the process themselves. Using their advice and the advice I found online, I was able to gain a number of interview invitations from nearly all of the programs I had applied to. After the interview process was complete, I finally chose to attend the BS/MD program that best fit my specific preferences: no MCAT required, a great scholarship package, not too far yet not too close to home, and non-binding (meaning I had the option of applying to a different medical school later without losing my seat in medical school). This process taught me not only how to apply and interview, but also how to set myself up for success in the years preceding senior year of high school.

Many people are not familiar with this field and need some help navigating this new road. I was fortunate enough to have received all of the right advice at the right time in terms of which programs to apply to and how to stay competitive, and that is why I have written this book. I want to share with students and parents —thoroughly — what it takes to get into these programs and how one can distinguish his/her application. I hope this book can serve as a "mentor" for you.

I know the road to becoming a doctor can be a difficult one. The traditional route to medical school is highly variable and thousands of eager pre-medical students do not gain admission despite competitive applications. That's why there is no better time than *now* (as a high school student) to secure your seat in medical school and maximize your chances early by utilizing all the resources and services provided on the website and in this book. Together, the book and the website complement each other very well. As a recent graduate of a combined medical degree program, I have included additional insight toward the end of the book that is often overlooked as a high school student. In fact, it is insight that I've only gained after going through the latter years of the program. I truly believe this book in its latest edition provides even more insight into the field of medicine. I hope that the hours I spent (and continue to spend) on this subject will save you hundreds of hours, so you can use your time doing things that matter to you most.

* * * * *

Introduction

This book is for those young adults in high school who either know they want to be doctors or who are considering it. My hope is that through reading this book, you will be able to discover if the field of medicine is a field you want to pursue and should you decide it is, how you can take advantage of a combined BS/MD program. By doing so, you'll be able to accomplish your dreams and do it in the shortest time possible. With proper planning, a combined Bachelors (B.S. or B.A.) & Medical Degree (M.D.) program allows you to gain admission into medical school from high school. These are commonly known as direct/combined/straight/guaranteed BS-MD or BA-MD programs. They can be as short as six years or seven years (at which point they are termed "accelerated"), or as long as eight years. At present (2019) there are approximately 67 such programs in the United States, out of the more than 140 accredited medical schools.

The Association of American Medical Colleges reported that in 2017 there were over 50,000 applicants to American medical schools—and each applicant had applied to approximately 14 medical schools! What percentage was accepted? While the percentage of applicants received into one of the top 10 US medical school can be as low as 2 percent, the national average is about 43 percent. The percentage of applicants admitted into the direct BS/MD programs varied from as low as 4 percent to as high as 11+ percent.

What are the advantages of the BS/MD program over the traditional route of first obtaining a four-year college degree and then applying to medical school? There are several, and we'll discuss them in detail. But one of biggest advantages lies in another name used for some programs: "guaranteed" admissions program. The

BS/MD program allows you to stay focused and go straight to your goal of becoming a physician, and, in the six- and seven-year programs, get there more quickly. Most programs have either a comparatively low MCAT score requirement to move on to the medical school, and some have no MCAT requirement at all. Often times in the traditional application route, it is one's inability to score well on these exams that delay, or prevent, one's admission into medical school.

If you know medicine is the career you want to pursue, we'll go through each piece of the puzzle to teach you how to be the most competitive applicant you can be. It is becoming increasingly tough to gain admission into these programs, but with the right advice and preparation, it can be you.

* * * * *

Advice for Parents and Other Adults

This book is not only for students, but for parents and other adults whose children or other significant young people in their lives feel inspired to become medical doctors. It is meant to be a basic reference for you to the realities of this goal, and, in some sense, an encouragement for its pursuit. If the young person in your life (as parent or other adult) has the intelligence, aptitude, desire, and commitment, then the next most important factor for them to succeed is your support and guidance. Almost every other practicality can likely be worked out, finances included. As an adult, you have the broader life experiences that can sometimes open doors to the aspiring doctor, such as in finding volunteer opportunities, arranging meetings and interviews with professionals involved in projects of potential interest, or arranging participation in health or medically-related evening or summer programs. In any case, as a minor, this young person will often need your permission to become involved in the projects and activities necessary to his or her own life experience related to the medical field—projects and activities essential for his or her eventual successful application to a BS/MD program.

In many households, parents are highly active in their child's decisions. More than any other group (political leaders, celebrities, etc), parents are considered the most influential in a child's decisions. A supportive and encouraging home environment goes a long way in helping a young person stay balanced and do his or her best.

* * * * *

Useful Terminology

- B.S. – Bachelor's of Science, for majors that have more science-based classes such as Biology, Physics, Chemistry, Psychology, Engineering, etc.
- B.A. – Bachelor's of Arts, for majors that are more liberal arts-based, including classes such as Political Science, English, History, Communications, etc.
- M.D. – Doctor of Medicine; this degree is conferred after completing medical school.
- Pre-med – a track that one takes before medical school in order to satisfy prerequisites for medical school, including organic chemistry, biology, and physics. This is not a major rather a track, meaning it includes all of the prerequisites generally needed to apply for medical school.
- Combined degree program – also called combined medical programs, direct BS/MD program, direct BA/MD program, straight medical programs, guaranteed admissions programs.
- Accelerated medical program – these programs are the same as combined or direct medical programs; however, they are completed in 6 or 7 years rather than the traditional 8 years.

* * * * *

What is the field of Medicine?

One of the things about a BS/MD program is that you're committing yourself to your future career in Medicine. One thing I've learned over the years is that many students enrolling in these programs do not understand the basics of the field of Medicine, and all that it entails. Don't worry, I was in this boat too. You learn a lot throughout your journey within the program, including what you enjoy doing, the types of patients you like seeing, and the type of life you want to live. While many of these questions you might not be able to answer as a high school student (or even if you can, it will inevitably change dozens of times), I've realized at the crux of it all, you have to love serving and helping others. Whether or not you like working with your hands is less relevant to decide whether medical school is for you. In a similar respect, knowing you like working only with elderly patients is also less relevant at this point. These are the kinds of questions you will need to inevitably answer toward the end of your medical school education. There is a special uniqueness to each field, which makes medicine inviting to so many different types of individuals. But again, the crux of it all has to be a passion to serve. The most incredible and successful physicians have this innate quality innate, and they tend to be the happiest.

But I think it is incredibly important and beneficial to know more about the field of medicine as it can give you a deeper understanding of all the amazing things you can do as a physician.

I briefly give an outline/oversight about the structure of your path as a physician below:

<u>The Journey</u>

- Bachelor's Degree (BA or BS), 2-4 years

Everyone requires a Bachelor's Degree before entering medical school. Whether it is Bachelor in Science (B.S.) or Bachelor of Arts (B.A.), it doesn't matter. You just need one.

- Medical School (MD), 4 years

It is during Medical School where you attain your Medical Degree. Another type of degree that allows you to be a physician is the D.O. degree (Doctor of Osteopathic Medicine). Ultimately, it is a different route to the same job. During medical school, you will take your Step 1 and Step 2 USMLE licensing exams. It is required that you pass these exams in order to match into a residency (see the next section). Beyond passing, doing well on these exams enables you to apply for more competitive residency positions.

- Residency, 1-7 years

This is the period during which you will train as a physician in your specific field, whether that is Family Medicine, General Surgery, Ophthalmology, Dermatology, or anything in between. Essentially, you will train to become the physician you will be for the rest of your career. During this period, you are termed a "Resident Physician." Upon completion, you become an "Attending Physician." Additionally, you will complete Step 3 of your USMLE Licensing exam during this period.

- Fellowship, 1+ years

After residency, you have the option to further subspecialize. You can subspecialize after nearly any residency. For example, if you are in an Internal Medicine residency, you can specialize in Cardiology for an additional 3-year fellowship. You can further sub-specialize within Cardiology (i.e. Interventional Cardiology, Electrophysiology) with an additional 1-year fellowship.

As mentioned previously, residency is the period during your career where you train to become the type of physician you wish to be (i.e. cardiologist, internist, dermatologist, ophthalmologist, anesthesiologist, etc). Residency is required in order to become a practicing physician. A residency can be between 1 and 7 years. Fellowship follows residency, and is usually the time at which one further sub-specializes. Almost every field has fellowships whereby physicians can sub-specialize. The field with the most fellowships is Internal Medicine (this is the path toward Cardiology, Pulmonology, etc - see list below).

Many times students are confused as to what kind of physicians they can be. The list is quite vast and varied and there is usually a fit for any type of student; throughout years 3 and 4 of medical school (during rotations), students will be able to identify what field they would like to go into. Unfortunately, there isn't nearly enough time to experience each of these specialties during medical school, so finding time as a high school student or an undergraduate student to shadow and understand each of these physicians' roles will help.

Here is a sample of some of the fields of medicine one can enter:

- Anesthesiology
- Dermatology
- Emergency Medicine
- Family Medicine
- General Surgery
- Internal Medicine *(see specialties below)*
  - Adult Critical Care
  - Allergy and Immunology
  - Cardiology
  - Endocrinology
  - Gastroenterology
  - Geriatric Medicine
  - Hematology/Oncology
  - Infectious Disease
  - Nephrology
  - Oncology
  - Pulmonology
  - Rheumatology
  - Sports Medicine
- Neurology
- Nuclear Medicine
- Obstetrics & Gynecology (OBGYN)
- Ophthalmology
- Orthopedic Surgery
- Pathology
- Pediatrics
- Plastic Surgery
- Psychiatry
- Radiation Oncology
- Radiology
- Transitional Year

A Brief History of Medical Schools and the Direct BS/MD Programs

Before the mid-1700s a person learned medical practice in the United States through apprenticeship, and, if he or she was really serious, found a way to study in the lecture halls and hospitals of the United Kingdom or on Continental Europe. America at the time had no standardized training and no certification. In 1765, the College of Pennsylvania started a series of formal lectures in the theory and practice of medicine. Then, in addition to one's apprenticeship, an aspiring doctor who had sufficient knowledge of Latin, mathematics, natural and experimental philosophy could obtain a bachelor's degree and be admitted for a one-year supervised program at the Pennsylvania Hospital.

In 1791 the University of Pennsylvania had already started its own medical school and brought the College of Pennsylvania program under its wing. Soon medical schools began popping up all over America; many were independent institutions, but, over time, only those associated with established colleges and universities proved viable. It was not until the end of the nineteenth century that serious qualifications for medical training were required. Notably, it was Johns Hopkins Medical School that established the requirement of a bachelor's degree for entrance into its medical program, followed by Harvard Medical School in 1901. In the early years of American medicine there were many types of doctors: medical doctors, naturopaths, homeopaths, osteopaths, and chiropractors, all of whom professed a certain approach or philosophy regarding healing. In 1847 medical doctors formalized their profession within the American Medical Association (AMA). For a variety of reasons, the AMA eventually became the dominant voice in the broader field of medical, healing, and pharmaceuticals. BS/MD programs are part of the medical approach that now characterizes American medicine, which is founded in the contemporary biological sciences and the experimental method of science altogether.

While the first BS/MD program in America appeared in the 1960s, now, approximately one-third of medical schools in the United States offer a combined BS/MD program to well-qualified high school students.

The advantages of applying to a direct BS/MD program from high school are many: 1) if you are accepted you know you have a seat waiting for you in medical school. Outside of the academic and professional requirements instituted at each individual program, you don't need to work above and beyond throughout undergrad to strengthen yourself up for a rigorous medical school application process; 2) you can explore majors and minors in fields outside of medicine (as long as your program permits) which can help you enter medical school more well-rounded and help you identify other interests; and 3) if for some reason you don't get accepted, you have a chance while in college to enhance your application and apply to medical school later. In other words, at least you tried to get in early on, and if you didn't get accepted into a program, you didn't waste any time in your life. As you will see, whatever academic qualifications there may be, preparation and persistence are key.

A direct BS/MD program guarantees your admission into medical school, contingent upon certain criteria specific to each program. The program is not a way around the necessity to do well, and you still must excel in your education. For some programs, as long as you maintain the appropriate grade point average (GPA), admission to their medical school is a given. For other programs, in addition to academic excellence, they also require a certain minimum performance on the Medical College Admission Test (MCAT). You would be surprised to learn that some programs do not require you to take the MCAT and others do not require a minimum score, thus relieving you of any stress you may feel during the process.

There may also be other requirements such as community service or health-care related volunteering. The beauty of these programs is that you know if you simply meet the requirements they have on paper, you're in; whereas with the traditional process of applying as an undergraduate, even with a great application, you may not gain admission into medical school.

Still, other programs create their own unique curriculum that merges BS and MD studies, so that you pursue both degrees simultaneously during the course of the program. One such program is the University of Missouri-Kansas City (UMKC) 6 Year BA/MD Program. You might find yourself taking a typical undergraduate class such as Organic Chemistry in the morning and then having a practice patient encounter simulation in the afternoon.

There are three basic forms of the direct BS/MD program:
    6-year program (accelerated & guaranteed)
    7-year program (accelerated & guaranteed)
    8-year program (guaranteed)

Obviously in each program you are going to learn everything you need to be a competent physician, so the shorter the program, the more intense it will be, including perhaps taking a heavier course load or attending summer sessions.

While the term BS/MD is often used throughout this book, some programs are a BA/MD program—which means there is a more liberal arts-focused curriculum in the undergraduate institution. These terms are used interchangeably as the requirements and experience are generally the same.

These programs have become increasingly more popular among high school students interested in medicine, yet in the grand scheme of things, still pretty arcane. The number of applications submitted to a specific program can range between the upper hundreds to lower thousands all for a handful or couple dozen seats. This may sound intimidating, but let's talk about ways in which you can maximize your chance of success.

* * * * *

What Does the Ideal Candidate Look Like?

By the time you are sending in the applications in your senior year of high school, your goal is to already look like the ideal candidate. In fact, every year it becomes harder to gain admission because more and more applicants look "ideal." What does "ideal" mean? Let's explore.

☞ How have you already shown your **interest in medicine**? Do you belong to any clubs related to health care or medicine? Do you volunteer in any health- or medicine-related organizations or institutions? Have you done any special research projects related to health or medicine? Have you taken any extra courses related to your interest in medicine? Do you have any health-related hobbies? You obviously need to prove "healthcare" is something you're not just interested in but also something you have been an active participant in (the latter proving the former). They want to make sure you've been involved in healthcare at some level to help prove your understanding of it and commitment to it.

☞ How **well-rounded** are your involvements? Your application is not just about being involved in everything related to "medicine," "healthcare," and "helping others." It's also about doing things that are personally interesting and meaningful to you. It's about learning more about your culture and sharing that with others. If you have been taking piano lessons since the 1st grade, great! That's something that should be listed on your resume and discussed at an interview. If you're involved with any personal enrichment activities, include that as well! More and more, the admissions committee wants to see a well-rounded applicant, not one that simply has a healthcare focus.

☞ How familiar are you with the entire field of medicine and the various types of practice and research? What have you done to familiarize yourself with medicine as a professional career? Have you shadowed or worked as a scribe?

☞ Do you know, and can you express clearly, **why you want to pursue a career in medicine**? Was there something that happened in your personal life or a moment where you witnessed the power of medicine? Perhaps it is actually that the practice of medicine correlates perfectly with something else you enjoy doing (i.e. solving puzzles. By the way, please don't use this one. It is one of the most overused!). This is going to be a huge question you'll have to answer over and over again, from your supplementary essays to interview day. They want to know why you chose medicine as a career.

☞ How do you feel you have proven both your interest in medicine and your ability to stay focused in your studies? What other qualities do you have that would make you a good physician? For example, are you in involved in research demonstrating your curiosity? Do you have qualities of a hard work ethic perhaps demonstrated by your grades or even *improving* your grades? You should have examples ready that can reflect each of these qualities.

☞ What are the ways you have demonstrated your **role as a leader**? What leadership activities do you have? It is ideal to have a few clubs or organizations you are a leader in. You don't need to be the President in each club, but you should have an important role and be able to describe why it was important. What were your roles and why were they meaningful? How did these roles enhance your character? What were the challenges you faced in this leadership position and how did you handle it and grow from it?

☞ How are your **academic grades**? Do you have a GPA of 3.5+?

☞ How are your **standardized test scores**? Do you at least have 1200+ SAT, 29+ ACT?

☞ Do you know people (other than your family and personal friends) who can attest to your interests, characteristics, and ability to persist and stay focused? You'll want to have **strong letters of**

recommendation from people you have worked alongside who can describe your personality and work ethic.

As you can see from the above questions, getting into a BS/MD program requires preparation and is not something that can be rushed in to a month before applications are due. You have to have already proven in your short few years of high school your unique interest in medicine as well as your ability to handle the academic demand. If you haven't yet accumulated enough experience, though, you may still have time. Review the timeline later in this book to see when you should begin your road to the combined medical program. If you feel you need more than that, drop us a line (hello@directbsmd.com) and we'll see how we can help further. Perhaps you might need someone to set up a timeline with you or answer any questions you may have about the process.

The ideal candidate for a BS/MD program will, first of all, be one hundred percent confident of his or her commitment to a medical career. This confidence will be obvious in many ways. First of all it will be shown by the candidate's knowledge of the medical field itself—not of the hard medical facts and science, but of the possibilities and realities of the medical profession. What is the day-to-day of a physician like? What are the hardships of going through medical school and how have you shown you can adapt? What are the rewards as a physician? How about the challenges in this career? Think about it this way: How can the admissions committee trust your confidence if they feel you don't know what you are committing to? The candidate should also be able to speak with intelligence about his or her knowledge and feelings about the various aspects of medicine, such as the real demand of study, the specialties the candidate may be considering, current public debate

23

regarding healthcare, and any interest in research or experimental medicine.

Part of this confidence will also be a clear, confident, and empathetic response to the question "why do you want to be a physician?" What has happened in your life that you have chosen medicine? *This will be asked!*

It is understood and well proven that the best predictor of future performance (and behavior) is past performance (and behavior). Therefore, the ideal candidate will already have a history of doing things that clearly demonstrate his or her persistent interest in the medical field. He or she will have some real life experience related to health and medicine, for example, volunteer work in a hospital or in some medically-related community service, observing physicians at work, working globally in a missions project, sitting in on courses at the local medical school, assisting in medically-related research projects at a local college or medical school, and so forth.

In the course of obtaining this life experience the candidate will have formed positive and supportive relationship with people working in the medical field who can attest to his or her genuine interest and aptitude for the medical field. These people will happily write honest and straightforward letters of recommendation for the candidate.

The candidate will also have a history of scholastic performance that demonstrates his or her ability to successfully meet the strenuous academic demands of the medical curriculum.

How smart does the ideal candidate have to be? Well, if at this point you are a high school sophomore, junior or senior and are seriously considering a BS/MD program, you should have pretty decent grades up in the higher quartiles of your class. As a sophomore with decent grades, you might still have a chance to turn the ship around with hard work and persistence (and studying extra hard for your standardized exams.) As a freshman, you have plenty of time to work hard and lay the groundwork for a successful high school career. Persistence is key. While IQ in the setting of BS/MD applications means nothing (fun fact: according to a 2002 report from the University of Wisconsin-Madison, the IQ of a medical doctor range between 116 and 134, with a median of 120), the ideal candidate will have performed well on certain standardized test (SAT/SATII/ACT). Not all programs require every test, and minimum scores required vary.

The following list gives you an idea of what is expected in general. The numbers below represent the general minimum (some programs do have lower minimums and averages) to begin looking into combined BS/MD programs.

In high school:
GPA 3.5+
SAT 1100+ (but on average ~1300)
ACT 29+
SATII Math and Science 650+
AP exams

For some BS/MD programs, it is required for the applicant to be a legal resident of the state. Sometimes, a legal resident of the state is preferred. This is not always the case, but in some states it is a significant factor in candidate selection.

* * * * *

List of BS/MD Programs in the United States

See the charts in this next section for requirements for specific programs. When looking into each university's program, look carefully to see how these qualifications apply specifically to each program. It is impossible to list every requirement that all the program's demand so research each one individually after coming up with a general list of which programs you qualify for (mainly based on state, SAT/ACT, GPA, ranking).

I provide a FREE resource at www.directBSMD.com, which has an updated list. These charts are accurate as of May 2019. We highly recommend viewing the online chart to see the full, updated list. (which also has hyperlinks to link you directly to the program's website). I also provided a list in this book in case you want to make notes. I try to update the list once a year, and closer to the summer (as that is when programs update their information). There may be some omissions or errors in these charts as the program's do not always update the website. Please contact programs directly with specific questions regarding their program.

More importantly, we would suggest visiting: https://www.aamc.org/students/applying/requirements/msar/, a website made by AAMC which includes a list of BS/MD programs available. While we found the list does leave out several programs, it is still worthwhile to visit the website. Note that there is a nominal fee to get access to this information for one full year.

Remember, starting now to plan your medical education is the surest way to maximize your possibility of getting into a program. Be systematic, organized, thorough, and above all, persistent.

Some instructions before viewing the chart:

- An * under UG (undergraduate) state denotes that the program has a preference to residents of that state or only those from that state are eligible. View program's website for complete details.

- If it is an "MCAT required" program, it will indicate a Yes/No. If Yes, a minimum score to attain may be shown. A mark of "DNM" means "**D**oes **N**ot **M**atter" what you score on the MCAT.

- - ** under SAT indicates the "average" SAT score of admitted students. (No asterisk = the minimum required).

- "Contact" means to contact the program regarding this information as it was not available at the time of data collection

- *Blanks or "n/a" in the table indicate that the information has not been made available. A "no" means not required. As you will recognize on the table, there is a handful of information not readily available on the program's website. If it is a program you are interested, feel free to contact the program director to ask your specific questions.*

- *Unlike previous editions, we removed three sections from the table (SAT II, Recommendation Letter requirements, and Program maintenance requirement) as we found that this information takes away from the purpose of the table – to find out which programs you qualify for.*

Review the most up-to-date program list online (with hyperlinks!) at www.directBSMD.com at your convenience.

6 Year Programs:

Program	UG State	Years	MCAT	SAT min.	ACT Min.	Rank/GPA	# accepted	Deadline
California Northstate University	CA	6,7,8	Yes:510	1400	31	3.75	10	Oct.31
Howard University	DC	6	Yes:504	1950	26	3.5	n/a	Contact
Texas JAMP	TX*	6	Yes: 499	1484	20.6	3.25	n/a	Oct.1
University of Missouri Kansas City	MO	6	No	1420	32	3.9	110+	Nov.1

7 Year Programs:

Program	UG State	Years	MCAT?	SAT Minimum	ACT Minimum	GPA/Rank	# accepted	Deadline
Albany Medical College	NY	7,8	Yes:510	n/a	n/a	3.5, 10%	45	Dec. 15
Augusta University	GA	7	Yes; no less than prior national mean	1400	32	3.7	n/a	Nov. 15
Boston University	MA	7	Yes	n/a	n/a	n/a	n/a	Nov. 15
Caldwell University	NJ	7, 8	Yes	1450	32	3.5	n/a	Jan. 15
California Northstate University	CA	6,7,8	Yes:510	1350	29	3.6	29	Oct.31
The College of New Jersey	NJ	7	No	1500+	34	4.5/5%	40	Dec. 1
CCNY CUNY Sophie Davis	NY*	7	No	req'd	req'd	85+	~60	Jan. 8
Drew University	NJ	7	Yes but dnm	1500	33	3.8/ 10%	5-10	Nov. 1
Grambling University	LA	7, 8	n/a	900	20	3.25	n/a	*Nov. 1
George Washington University	DC	7	No	1400+	90% percentile	n/a	n/a	Nov.15
Florida Atlantic University	FL	7,8	Yes:510	1490	33	4.3	n/a	Jan.11
Lehigh University	PA	7	n/a	1300	30	3.3, 10%	n/a	Jan. 1
Marshall University	WV	7	No	1390	>30	3.75	n/a	Jan.15
Miami University	FL	7, 8	Yes	1300	31	3.7/10%	n/a	Nov. 1
Montclair University	NJ	7	Yes but dnm	1100 (550 in both CR & Math in one sitting)	32+	B*/10%	n/a	Dec.1
New Jersey Institute of Technology	NJ	7	n/a	1490 (one sitting)	33 (one sitting)	Highest	13	Nov. 15
Northwestern University	IL	7,8	No	792** (Math), 762** (Read)	35 Composite, 11 Writing	No cut-off, but should be at the top	n/a	Jan. 1
Penn State	PA	7	Yes:504	1470	32	Highest 10%	25	Nov.1
Rosemont College	PA	7,8	Yes: 500	1150	31	3.4/25%	n/a	Jan. 1
Rutgers University	NJ	7,8	Yes, but dnm	1400	32+	3.5, 10%	n/a	Nov.1

28

Rensselaer Polytechnic Institute	NY	7	No	1471	n/a	n/a	n/a	Nov.1
St. George's University	NJ	7	Yes but dnm	1270	32+	3.5, 10%	n/a	Dec.1
The City College of New York	NY	7	n/a	Avg. 85%	n/a	n/a	n/a	Jan. 8
University of Illinois-Chicago	IL*	7, 8	Yes: 510	>1310	>28	3.85/15%	43-55	Nov.1
University of South Alabama	AL	7	n/a	1260 (in-state)/ 1360 (out-state)	27(in-state)/30(out-state) one sitting	2.5(in-state)/3.5(out-state)	n/a	Dec.15
University of Toledo	OH	7, 8	No	1310	28	3.5	5	Dec. 1
Temple University	PA	7,8	Yes: 508	n/a	n/a	3.8	n/a	Nov. 1
Oklahoma University	OK	7	Yes:508	1390	30	3.75, 10%	5 to 8	Jan.14
University of South Florida	FL	7	Yes: 515	1470	33	4	avg.15	Aug. 1
UT Health San Antonio	TX*	7	Yes	1300	29	3.75	n/a	Dec.1

8 Year Programs:

Program	UG State	Years	MCAT?	SAT Minimum	ACT Minimum	Rank/GPA	# accepted	Deadline
Baylor University	TX	8	500-507	1430	32	3.7, 5%	6	Jan. 19
Brooklyn College	NY	8	Yes	1300-1450	n/a	n/a	15	Dec 15
Brown University	RI	8	No	2200	n/a	no specific requirement	60	Nov. 1
Caldwell University	NJ	7, 8	Yes	1400	32	3.5	n/a	Jan. 15
California Northstate University	CA	6,7,8	Yes:510	1250	29	3.5	27	Oct.31
Case Western Reserve University	OH	8	No	2200-2300	31-34	10%	15-20	Dec. 1
Drexel University	PA	8	Yes	1360	31	3.5/10%	n/a	Nov. 1
Duqesne University	PA	8	Yes	1240	26 in one sitting	3.5	5	Apr.1
Fisk University	TN	8	Yes:24	n/a	High	3.2	n/a	Early Jan.
Florida Atlantic University	FL	7,8	Yes:510	1490	33	4.3	n/a	Jan.11
Grambling University	LA	7, 8	n/a	900	20	3.25	n/a	n/a
Hofstra University	NY	8	Yes: (Equivalent to 80th %ile one sitting)	1410	32	3.7; top 10%	n/a	Nov. 15/Dec. 15
Loyola University Chicago	IL	8	Yes:509	n/a	n/a	3.5	10	Aug.24
Mercer University	GA	8	n/a	1390	30	3.7	18	Jan.9
Miami University	FL	7, 8	Yes	1300	31	3.7/10%	n/a	Nov. 1
Monmouth University	NJ	8	Yes but dnm	1300	29+	10%	n/a	Dec. 1
Northwestern University	IL	7, 8	No	792** (Math), 762** (Read)	35 Composite, 11 Writing	No GPA requirement, but should be at the top	n/a	Jan. 1

				Avg: 745 (CR), 760 (Math), 745 (Writing)				
Rice University	TX	8	Yes	Avg: 745 (CR), 760 (Math), 745 (Writing)	Avg. 33.5	Top 5%	6	Dec. 1
Rosemont College	PA	7,8	Yes: 500	1150	31	3.4/25%	n/a	Jan. 1
Siena University	NY	8	No	1360	30+	10%	12-14	Nov.1
South Alabama University	AL*	8	Yes: 504	1260(in-state), 1360(out-of-state)	27(in-state), 30(out-of-state)	3.5	n/a	Dec.15
St. Bonaventure University	NY	8	No	1390	30	90+	up to 15	Dec. 1
St. George's University	NJ	8	Yes: 498	n/a	n/a	3.3	n/a	Contact
St. Louis University	MO	8	Yes but dnm	1390	30+	> B in science classes	n/a	Dec. 1
Stonybrook University	NY	8	Yes:above natnl avg	1490-1590	NO	3.4, 98-99%	n/a	Jan. 15
SUNY Upstate - Adelphi University	NY	8	No	1360	29	90%/3.5	n/a	Dec. 1
SUNY Upstate - Albany College of Pharmacy and Health Sciences	NY	8	No	1360	31	90%	5	Nov.15
SUNY Upstate - University at Albany	MA	8	No	1360	29	3.5	10	Dec. 1
SUNY Upstate - Hampton University	VA	8	No	1360	31	90%	5	Nov.1
SUNY Upstate - Purchase College	NY	8	No	1360	29	90%	10	Nov.15
SUNY Upstate - Yeshiva University	NY	8	No	1360	29	90%	5	Nov.1
University of Alabama-Birmingham	AL	8	Yes:506	1400	30+	3.5	14	Dec.17
University of Oklahoma	OK	7	Yes:508	1390	30	3.75, 10%	5 - 8	Jan. 8
University of Cincinnati	OH	8	Yes	1300+	29+	no	n/a	Jan.10
University of Colorado-Denver	CO*	8	Yes	1185+	27+	3.5	10	Oct.26
University of Connecticut	CT	8	Yes:80th percentile	1350	29	3.5	n/a	Dec. 1
University of Delaware	DE	8	Yes:504(no section < 126)	1800(Approx)	n/a	3.5	15	Contact
University of Evansville	IN*	8	Yes	1350	29	4	8	Nov. 1
University of Illinois-Chicago	IL*	7, 8	Yes:510	equivalent	34	3.5, 15%	43-56	Dec. 1
University of Nevada	NV*	8	Yes	1320	28	3.7, 10%	approx. 15	Jan. 22
University of New Mexico	NM*	8	Yes: 491	>=510	22 in math, 19 in other subsections	3.37	28	Nov. 13
University of Pittsburgh	PA	8	No	1490	34	Highest GPA at their school	8 - 12	Dec. 1
University of Rochester	NY	8	No	high	high	3.95; 3%	<10	Nov. 15
University of Texas-Rio Grande Valley	TX*	8	Yes: 498	1500(3 Part)	21	3.5	n/a	Jan 22.
University of Toledo	OH	7, 8	No	1310	28	3.5	5	Dec. 1

University of the Sciences	PA	8	Yes: 508	1150	25	3.5, 25%	4	Dec. 11
Virginia Commonwealth University	VA	8	Yes:502	1330	29+	3.5	15	Nov.15
Washington and Jefferson College	PA	8	Yes: 508	1350	31	5%	n/a	Dec.10
Washington University St. Louis	MO	8	Yes: 97 percentile	n/a	n/a	3.8, *5%	n/a	Jan 2
Wayne State University	MI	8	Yes	1310	28	3.5	10	Dec.1
Westchester University	PA	8	Yes	1240	n/a	3.5, top 10%	n/a	Nov. 14

Visit www.directBSMD.com for hyperlinks to each program's
website and for updated information, and for
the most up-to-date information.

Notes

Note

Which Programs Should I Apply To &

Which Program Should I Choose?

The answer to this question depends on a number of factors, and for some, the answer may be "whichever program will accept me." More competitive applicants may have more options to choose from and the option to be a bit more "picky" in terms of what they want from a program. Less competitive applicants might simply be focused on gaining admission into *any* program that will take them. Regardless, once you have more than one offer, you need to weigh a few factors. If you end up with just one offer, before accepting, you want to seriously consider if this program is one that will be a good fit for you. You don't want to accept the offer just because it is the only one you've received. Throughout your application or interview process, you may be asked "Why is our program right for you?" You'll want to have specific aspects of the program you love and are genuinely excited to become part of. You'll need to prepare a considered response.

By the time applicants are deciding between various acceptances, most applicants inherently can decipher which program is best for them and their families. Going with your gut feeling about how well you get along with other students and faculty in the program on interview day is going to be a big key. Go where you feel you will be best supported and ultimately, become the best doctor you can! Here are some additional considerations to take into account when picking programs to apply to and which to ultimately attend.

✓____ Which schools do you qualify for academically? There is no need to apply to many competitive schools if you're GPA and exam scores don't meet their averages. However, it doesn't mean you shouldn't apply. It is always a good idea to select several programs that are "reach" schools (where your qualifications are below average for the program). You never know – you may actually get an interview from them. Another thing to consider is if you were in this rigorous learning environment, do you feel like you could succeed? In contrast, attending a school whose entrance requirements are below *your* qualifications may limit your opportunities later for residency or other post-graduate training. Do you want to be the big fish in a small pond or a small fish in a big pond? There is no right answer, and everyone is unique in this regard. Each scenario has its own advantages. If you're in a less competitive program associated with a lesser-known medical school, your probability to be at the top of the class will be higher. Conversely, a more competitive program with a well-known medical school may challenge you academically and might make it harder for you to be at the top of the class. It is *very* important to note that these are broad generalizations, and with the appropriate effort, diligence, and determination, there is no reason you cannot be at the top of the class in a challenging medical school (after all, someone needs to be there!). I would always recommend putting yourself in an environment where there are others to challenge you so you can always strive to become even better than you already are. Educational excellence is always about getting better and improving. If you're already at the top, there is no room to improve, right?

✓____ How balanced is the list of programs I am applying to? We talked above about "reach" programs. But you'll want to also include "match" and "safety" programs. I'd encourage you to have several in each of these 3 categories. The "match" programs are those who are looking for applicants with a GPA/SAT/ACT score (more or less) similar to yours, as evidenced by the "average applicant" numbers on their website. These statistics may not always be readily available online, so feel free to contact the program coordinator to find out what their average applicant's stats are. You can also gauge this based on meeting their minimum requirements. The "safety" programs should be those whose requirements or average applicant statistics are below your own statistics. In other words, you would have a "leg up" applying to these programs and acceptance should be a bit easier (relatively speaking). Depending on your career goals, I'd encourage those that perhaps are less competitive to also broaden their applications to include direct BS/DO (or osteopathic) programs as well. More on these programs later.

✓_____ Does the medical school have any special programs that you are interested in? For example, you may be interested in becoming a physician that works with cancer patients (i.e. hematology-oncology or radiation oncology) and so it would be ideal to attend a medical school with a cancer center. Or perhaps you have specific interests such as emergency medicine or trauma medicine, so going to a medical school with a Trauma 1 center would be ideal. If you know early on what you want to specialize in, it is easier to do research and set yourself up for success if your university is a research hub for your specific interests. If you don't know early on what you want to specialize in, don't worry at all. Most don't and if they do, they often change their mind a dozen times throughout medical school anyway. I know I did! It is very difficult, if not impossible, to expose yourself to and understand the ins and outs of the various medical specialties available to train in. It is wise to express in your essay and your interview that "X" BS/MD program is a huge attraction for you because of the "Y" and "Z" features.

✓_____ Is there a particular faculty member you would like to associate with? For example is there a professor doing specialized transplant procedures, or reconstructive surgery, or high tech imaging whose work you would like to participate in?

✓____ Does the school have program and curriculum flexibility that will allow you to study a major of your choice or allow you to study abroad for a semester? Undergraduate students often times find studying abroad for a semester one of the most memorable aspects of their undergraduate career. Given the time in your schedule and the financial resources, I'd highly recommend this!

✓____ Is the program binding or non-binding? In other words, are you able to apply out to different medical schools upon completing your pre-med prerequisites, or are you barred from applying out. If you can apply out and choose to, is your seat saved for you regardless of the result of the application process? This is important because you may want to take the MCAT (if not already required by the program), and if you do very well, you may want to try to apply to medical schools that are perhaps more prestigious or perhaps closer to home. The reason this is extremely important is because of the following: You can try to "apply out" to other medical schools during your senior year of undergrad if you wish, and – worse comes to worse – if you don't gain admission to any medical schools, It is nice to know that your program's affiliated medical school seat is still waiting for you.

✓____ How is the university rated? Is it well-known? A university's prestige can certainly be a factor you may use in picking a program to attend, especially if it is a non-binding program. This is because if you attempt to apply out, coming from a well-known university can help your medical school application.

✓____ Is the school in the state where you live? Many schools are state colleges and admit mostly (or only) residents of their state. Also, tuition can be many times higher for an out-of-state student. Finances are a huge aspect to consider when choosing which programs to apply to or attend. $30,000 per year for an in-state student versus $45,000 for an out-of-state student might seem like only a $15,000 difference. But multiply this difference across 4 or 8 years and now that's something to consider. If you're taking loans for your education, add the interest that will accrue each year and you may find yourself in a considerable amount of debt. When you have multiple program acceptance offers, finances should definitely be a consideration. When your options are more limited and becoming a physician has always been your dream, money shouldn't necessarily stop you, especially if you are borrowing conservatively. There are government loans that can support you through tuition and boarding. While there are student loan forgiveness plans that can help you to pay back (and even forgive!) your loans once you start practicing, it is always best to plan to avoid any loan as much as you can.

✓____ What will your finances allow you to do? For example, will you have to live at home and commute to college or need to live on campus and possibly forego the cost of a vehicle? Some students and families prefer for the student to be close to home. Others don't mind either way. These have huge financial implications as well when you take the cost of housing into account. Keep in mind that someone (either the student or parent) will likely be traveling often to visit, which also has some financial implications. As mentioned previously, finances should be a serious part of the consideration.

✓____ What is your budget for applying to the BS/MD programs? Each application requires sending your transcripts and standardized test scores and, if asked to come for an interview, travel costs. Remember, you definitely need to apply to an assortment of programs, but you certainly don't need (or want) to apply to every program in the country. When it comes to the budget for the actual application process, the overall cost of each application is significantly less than the downstream costs of having to apply to medical school later on. After you have a decent number of offered interviews, a number that you're personally comfortable with to maximize your chance of gaining admission after an interview, then you can choose to decline interviews if your personal finances of traveling don't permit. This number will vary for each person depending on how confident they are about their application as well as their interview skills. Remember the "safety," "match" and "reach" programs. I'd at least recommend applying to several in each category.

✓_____ Are there programs that have affirmative action goals or that reserve places for any special category of applicant, be it ethnicity, financial status, economically disadvantaged, and so forth, for which you qualify? Some programs were created specifically for those that are in under-represented backgrounds.

✓_____ Are there programs that have scholarships or financial aid for which you may qualify? Consider that you will be at this program for six to eight years – so ideally you would want to minimize the cost of each year (or at least during undergrad) so you don't leave medical school with an enormous debt. In-state residents also receive in-state tuition fees, and this may become a big factor when you're entering medical school. On average, medical students can walk out with over $200,000 in debt, and this number is rising every year. Going to a university that gives you scholarships (especially for your undergraduate years) will be a huge financial blessing down the line.

✓_____ What is the overall feel for the campus? What are the people like? Is this environment one you can find yourself being happy in? Does the university offer things you particularly enjoy, such as a new library, gym, etc? When you do get interview calls, make sure to go on a tour of the campus to really get a feel for the environment you'll be spending the next chapter of your life. Often times the interview day will consist of a tour, anyway so a separate tour wouldn't be necessary. A few campuses I visited have disappointed me. For most, this won't be a prime deciding factor, but could help with tiebreakers.

By going through the above checklist, you'll be able to make an informed decision on which programs to apply for and which to ultimately choose. The above are some of the predominant factors that helped me in my decision. Don't be afraid to reach out to current students or faculty either on the day of the interview or after. Most program directors are happy to share the emails of current students, so you can learn more about their experience. Don't be afraid to ask!

* * * * *

BS/MD vs. Traditional Pre-med Route

It's a valid question - **Why go the BS/MD route over the traditional pre-med route?** We'll go over some of the factors you'll want to consider.

The direct medical program route is for those that *know* they want to become a doctor. These programs provide a strong assurance that you'll be accepted into medical school compared to the traditional route. With the combined BS/MD medical program route, all you need to do is maintain your program's requirements (GPA, volunteer hours, perhaps a minimum MCAT score) and then you've gained admission into a medical school. All the additional stresses and headaches that come with applying to medical school are put aside.

With the traditional route, you'll have to work extremely hard to make sure you have great extracurricular experiences (volunteering, research, leadership, etc) as well as a great GPA and awesome MCAT score - and even with that, you *still* aren't necessarily guaranteed a spot in medical school. So many people have to take gap years after their undergraduate education to further boost their résumé in hopes of reapplying and gaining admission to medical school.

The guarantee of having a seat saved for you in medical school allows you to spend time during your undergraduate education to explore new interests or hone present interests. It allows you to do these things without the pressure of knowing "I have to do this to look more competitive for medical school applications." It may also allow you to explore a Major or Minor in a field you would have previously discounted or ignored. Although not recommended, it will even allow you to just do the bare minimum that the direct medical program requires to gain admission. In other words, you can coast through your undergraduate years more easily than if you were to be a traditional applicant. Again, this latter reason is not recommended because: a) you should always try to enhance yourself and explore new fields; b) exploring new fields will give you a new perspective on life and make you more well-rounded; c) these experiences will allow you to ultimately better connect with your future patients; d) medicine is a field of life-long learning; and e) you may discover a new passion.

Here are the facts. Direct medical programs are not known by many. Thus, the number of people applying are far less than the number of people applying to medical school. Even adjusting for the fact that there are less spots nationally in straight medical programs versus medical schools nationally, one has a higher chance of getting into a straight medical program over a medical school through the traditional route.

While I can go on and on about this - just know that if you want to pursue a career in medicine, the BS/MD path is the most guaranteed way. *Some would say the most guaranteed way is the best way.*

How to Do Well in High School

Doing well in high school is not just about getting good grades and doing all the practical things necessary to be accepted into a BS/MD program. Doing well in high school is also about maturing as a person, discovering more about who you are and becoming more aware of the world around you. It is in this environment where you will need to learn to deal with the challenges of working as a team member or a team leader, dealing with interpersonal conflicts, assessing your weaknesses and finding ways to overcome them, enhancing your strengths, and helping to build up others around you. With that being said, the following are some suggestions from myself, counselors and psychologists on how to do well in high school.

☞ Grades are important, but do not worry too much about them to the point it paralyzes you from doing other activities. The highest priority among these activities is making sure you have time for yourself to do things that will recharge you. For some it will be reading a book or playing sports, and for others it might be playing video games or watching a movie. It doesn't entirely matter what it is but it does matter that there is something. Time-management will be a huge key to balance what should be a busy four years in high school. You do have to get excellent grades, but know you are smart enough to achieve these grades so as long as you are able to discipline yourself to study as much as you need to. "There is nothing that I cannot learn" has always been a good mantra. With this attitude you will have time for other activities—activities that will help you grow as a person. If you are struggling to get good grades, try to get a coach or tutor to help you efficiently and effectively manage your time. If you find yourself struggling in certain subjects, definitely reach out to your teachers, other peers, or even hire a private tutor. Your goal is to be the best learner you can be, even if it requires the help of a tutor.

☞ Find out what relaxes you. You need to know how to de-stress. Maybe it's sports, maybe it's music, maybe it's a certain TV show, maybe it's playing chess, maybe it's just spending time with friends, maybe it's a certain kind of study that's not in the curriculum, maybe its meditation or yoga. You will need breaks from time to time, so don't worry about "wasting" time taking them, just make sure you get them when you need to. (Interviewers typically ask what you do to relax given your intense high school curriculum, in order to assess if you will understand the importance of taking care of yourself during the rigors of medical school ahead). During the interview, they actually enjoy hearing that you take time out of your busy week to de-stress.

☞ Understand the difference between quality and quantity in your study. Learn what really interests you about any particular subject. Your interest in a certain aspect of it will actually help you learn more about the subject as a whole. There are many approaches to any subject, some require more rote learning than others, but most all will have something that you can find particularly interesting. You may find it interesting to read the history of any particular subject. It is always interesting to read the biography (or autobiography) of one of the great men or women in any field. If you do, you will certainly find out what made the field interesting to them and how that interest turned into an important contribution to the world.

☞ Learn how to ask for help when you need it. Getting used to interacting with your teachers and counselors helps prepare you for relating to the adults you will meet as part of preparing for and getting into college and medical school. Teachers and counselors actually enjoy when you talk to them! Additionally, the better your relationship with them, the better your recommendation letters will look when it comes down to applying for these programs. Your recommendation letters of course should talk about how well you did in the class and how "academically intelligent" you are, but touching on personal traits like "curiosity" and "motivation" will help a lot.

☞ Stay healthy and physically active. Get enough sleep. If you have a particular interest in health and physical conditioning, you can even look for ways to get specialized instruction or research opportunities such as in nutrition, sports, martial arts, yoga and so forth. Also, try to get involved in sports in high school. Even if you don't want to commit to sports every year, trying it for a semester or two will show to colleges that you've at least experimented. No one is requiring you to enjoy it – and that's fine. But you never know, you may find a passion for running or volleyball along the way (like I did!).

☞ Don't worry about popularity. Make friends with other students who have similar interests as you. You will appreciate more having a few close friends than seeming to be well-liked by many who don't really know you. Having friends that have similar interests as you will help to keep you motivated academically. "You become what you surround yourself with." These close friends of yours will also remind you of deadlines you might have otherwise...overlooked.

☞ Learn how to set goals for yourself, make schedules, and discipline yourself. It isn't unreal or strange to set up an hour-by-hour plan for each day of the week in high school. Have long-term and short-term goals. Perhaps you want to become a leader for the Service Club by the end of the year; know what steps you need to take in advance and show your commitment to the club by getting highly involved in it. Nothing shows commitment and excitement for a club than constantly getting involved.

☞ Stretch your brain and other talents. Play with software and computer apps that, in a fun or challenging way, teach you how to think logically, or test your creativity, or force you to "think out of the box." Or consider picking up an instrument and learning to play. Perhaps you could even learn to sew or knit! The more you experiment now with what you enjoy doing, the better it'll come off during an interview. Additionally, these hobbies might help in drawing parallels between what you enjoy doing (your hobby) and what you want to do in the future (practice medicine). Again, interviewers want to see that you know what interests you, and you do what interests you. Sometimes, this unique interest of yours will be the only thing discussed during an interview!

The Standardized Tests

At some point in high school you will have to take certain standardized tests. Needless to say, successful candidates generally have very good scores. Some programs may require a SAT score as low as 1100 (on the new SAT) while others historically accept those with a 1350+. Some programs look at ACT scores as well depending on what part of the country you are from. You will need an ACT score of at least 26, but most applicants score 30+. The SAT/ACT requirement for a program does not necessarily reflect how competitive that program is. Contrary to popular belief, most programs do not simply cross your name off the list because your GPA/SAT didn't make it to the top 100 of that program's applicants. Some programs simply require a minimum for you to apply, and then begin weeding out the applicants based on which essay or application is better – not GPA/SAT. Ultimately, the interview will be the final deciding factor as to whom they admit.

Your GPA should be very competitive as many students will apply with a 90+ average (3.5+). Sometimes SATIIs are required in Math and Science and those scores should ideally be over 650+. I would advise you to take SATIIs in at least Math II and Biology-M. Consider SAT preparation companies to help you prepare for the test as they may help to improve your score. Some of these programs offer guarantees so it may be worth your time to consider them. However, you definitely do not need these companies to score well. Many people are very successful studying on their own by creating a study schedule and sticking to it.

Notice there is a difference between "average" and "minimum" as stated on programs' websites. Minimum requirements are strict. If you do not meet the minimum necessary GPA/SAT, then the program will automatically reject you. However, many programs have begun removing requirements and are now displaying "averages" on their websites of the previously admitted year. This means that if the previous year's admitted class' SAT average was a 1350, you can still apply if you have a lower score (i.e. 1250) – because an average obviously means that some have gotten scores below 1350 and some above. This program may be your "reach" program if your scores are below their average. If you are below average for any of the standardized tests or GPA for a particular program, this should not stop you from applying. Many admissions committees easily overlook shortcomings if a candidate is otherwise accomplished. There have been stories of people with bare minimum stats (GPA of 90 and SAT of 1200) who have written eloquent essays, dazzled on their in-person interviews, and thereafter gained admission into very competitive BS/MD programs.

Again, try to get rid of the notion that selection committees automatically sort people based on their SAT/GPA and then choose the top 50 to interview. This is not the case. The majority of programs (if they have a minimum SAT score of XYZ and you meet that minimum requirement) will look at your overall package. Of course, the lower your SAT score, the better your essays and resume needs to be to make up for it. The selection committees need a reason to choose someone with a 1250 over someone with a 1400, and your essays as well as the things you've done during your high school years can show them just what that reason is. In other words, if your GPA/SAT are on the lower end of the average, give them a reason to choose you over someone else. It took more than just one hole to sink the Titanic; the same can be applied for your application process.

The Essentials: Volunteering, Shadowing, Research, Relationships, and More

This section used to be titled: "The Extras," but in reality, these are now "essentials" for your application. Now that your foundation is set (i.e. standardized tests and GPA), the "essentials" are the make or break of getting into a BS/MD program. The essential are the life-level, tangible proofs of your genuine interest in and commitment to medicine. Regardless of natural talent or intelligence, the student has to really endeavor or apply him/herself in order to do these essentials, and it is this that puts you in the best position to be a successful applicant. Through these essentials, your decision to pursue medicine gets tested, and you prove to both yourself and the admissions committee that you know the career your are pursuing. You develop confidence in yourself and they develop confidence in you.

Volunteering

This section will be split up in to "Community Service" volunteering and "Medically-related" volunteering. Make sure you have plenty of meaningful volunteer experience you can talk about in your admission essays and during interviews.

Community Service Volunteering

This describes an activity where you volunteer for a non-medically related service. These include things like volunteering at a soup kitchen, a community cultural event, or any other type of national or local event where you are not working in health care or working with "patients." These types of experiences are important to have on top of your medically related service activities. Doing community service shows that you are not just focused on health care but also focused on donating your time to the community in general. You should try to have some sort of monthly or bimonthly commitment to a community service volunteer activity.

Medically-related Volunteering

This type of volunteer experience is one where you are working in health care or working with "the sick." It is important to note that the volunteering you do here should, in some way, open your eyes further to the field of medicine. Colleges do not want to hear about how fast you were able to file a patient's charts, rather they want to hear about the relationships you formed and how volunteering helped affirm your passion to become a physician. Most of the time, applicants use volunteering as a major reason for wanting to pursue a career in medicine. So when you initially begin volunteering, sign up for a position that will give you worthwhile experiences to discuss in your essays and interviews.

I want to take a quick moment aside to say that while you should have these life-guiding experiences so you can talk about it during your interviews, you also want to have these experiences for yourself. Going into medicine is a very long journey, and burnout can become real during medical school and residency. You owe it to yourself to find a true interest in the field. Having a passion in your heart for the field is incredibly important, much more important than showing your passion on your resumé.

Start volunteering in your freshman year of high school. The earlier the better, but if you cannot until eleventh grade for whatever reason, you can still set yourself up for success – don't worry. Keep reading. Some hospitals, depending on where you are from, don't allow volunteers to begin until the age of 16, which is OK. The options you have then are to either look for another hospital or fill your time doing something else demonstrating your understanding of patient-physician interactions or serving the sick. You could even consider going on a mission trip locally or internationally. When enrolling for volunteering, make sure you express interest to the hospital early, as there may be a long waitlist. For summer volunteering, it's beneficial to find out as early as the prior December or January. It is always better to be early than late as the worst someone will tell you is "You're too early." That is a much easier scenario to deal with than: "Sorry, you're too late and all our spots are filled for this year. Check in with us again next year."

Most of the time, the quality of your hours is more important than the quantity of your hours. However, the more the better. Some programs specifically want to see that you've had extensive experience in the hospital environment. Such programs may look for applicants with 300-400 hours! The reason that many hours is sometimes important is because the programs want to see that you've spent enough time in the hospital to really know that you want to be a doctor. They want to admit only those they know who will be unwavering in their pursuit of becoming a physician. Not someone who wants it simply as a security net. If you were to hire someone to drive a car from the east coast to the west coast, would you hire someone that is committed to the pursuit, or someone that might stop somewhere in the middle and drive somewhere else, or worse – give up? You want the most committed person for this task, and so does the BS/MD application committee. Additionally, it's important to be consistent. Set aside a few hours every week for volunteering. Try to volunteer at one or two hospitals without changing around too much; consistency and commitment are important to foster meaningful experiences and relationships. Make sure to document your volunteering history on your résumé.

Shadowing
Shadowing is an important piece you do not want to neglect. Along the same lines of volunteering, colleges want to see that you have experience in the hospital environment and know what the job of a

physician entails. Having direct shadowing experience will not only help you with your admission essays and interview but it will show that you have directly experienced the health care field and the patient-doctor relationship. Even for yourself, it may help you narrow which field of medicine you are interested in. A well-written essay could convey how this experience made you want to become a physician. Current practicing physicians also are a great resource for you to ask about their profession – which will soon be your profession.

Students often ask how to find doctors to shadow. You can simply look online and search for doctors at the nearest university hospital and either call or email them letting them know who you are and why you would like to shadow them (don't say that you need this experience to get into a medical program; rather mention that you are interested in the field of medicine and want to see if it is something you want to spend your life doing). You can also try to reach out to a program coordinator within a department (since their emails may be more accessible) and ask about shadowing a physician within the department. You could even ask your own doctor if you may shadow him/her on a few select days or if he/she knows any doctors that would be willing to allow you to shadow them. Any doctor you know will be more inclined to say yes. You don't need to shadow a doctor the way you would volunteer. A good timeline for shadowing is weekly, for 8-12 weeks. Any number of weeks above or below that is perfectly fine. But don't stop shadowing after that. Move on to another physician in another field of medicine. Since medicine is such a diverse field, it would be ideal to shadow primary care physicians, hospitalists, surgeons, and emergency medicine physicians. This way, you can get a taste of all the different specialties in medicine, one of which might connect closely to your own interests. Also, avoid shadowing family members but perhaps they can connect you with their colleagues.

You can include the physicians and their specialties you've shadowed on your resume as well. Make sure to foster a good relationship with these physicians since they may be a good source for a recommendation letter.

Do Research

Yes, even in high school you can do legitimate medical research. Research helps to demonstrate your curiosity and intellect. While BS/MD programs generally do not require candidates to have done research, to do so is a big plus that sets you apart from, and likely ahead of, many otherwise equally qualified candidates. Research helps students develop critical reasoning skills that aid science majors in their pursuit for higher education.

Some students research throughout their high school career while others apply for summer programs through a research facility or college university. The NIH offers some highly reputable research programs for students to get involved with over the summer. Increasingly, more and more students are conducting research, so its great if you can do it. An on-line search for "high school medical research" or "summer research programs for high school students" will bring up the many existing programs. If your high school does not have a science research program, then summers are the best time for you to research because it often requires nearly a full-time commitment for a few months. The ultimate goal for any research project is an abstract, poster, or publication (the latter being the most favored). It isn't necessary, but it is looked upon favorably.

Whatever research you can become involved with will be an important addition to your résumé. More and more, students are distinguishing themselves, and research offers one such way to do so. Work hard, be persistent, and try to get your research study published. This will not only help leverage you into a program, but it will also help you tremendously throughout your career. You should be able to speak intelligibly about your research and/or publication during your interviews.

Build Relationships

BS/MD applications require several letters of recommendation. Thus, it is important that you forge and foster relationships with teachers, community leaders, doctors, or research mentors so that they can write about positive traits that cannot be seen from your résumé. You should not request letters from family, even if you shadowed them. Every letter should talk about a different aspect of your character so that colleges can know you on a personal and professional level. Some recommendations could address, for example, how personable and empathetic you are while others could discuss your curiosity and perseverance. Your references will likely first want to speak with you about their recommendation, including what might be good for them to say, perhaps why you selected them for a reference, and what your future plans are. These are opportunities for honest and forthright conversations. With such conversations, your references will be able to write an effective letter for you.

Be sure to provide your references with ample information about yourself as well, such as your résumé and personal statement, which might attest further to how committed you are to the medical field. This will also help your references provide more personal and knowledgeable feedback about you. Give them ample time to write the letters. Typically you will want to request one from your teachers as early as the summer before your senior year, and as late as September of your senior year. For others in the community or research mentors, ask them soon after your last encounter with them so you are "fresh in their head." The earlier they know, the more receptive they will be to the idea because they'll be able to effectively manage their time with a long heads-up. Don't forget, they're also going to write dozens of recommendation letters for other students as well, so be respectful and understanding throughout the process.

Do More

This title was intentionally very vague. As mentioned earlier, people are distinguishing themselves more and more making it harder to choose you over applicant #605. Do something different to give them a reason to choose you. For example, getting EMT-B training isn't a stretch. That'll give you real life, hands-on experiences to show your passion to help others. I have seen some great essay written about this experience. Perhaps you're into leadership and change – ever think about starting your own non-profit organization? Of course this involves a lot of paperwork and might take several months to find the right managing team to help you and to get the word out about your organization, but it could be worth it depending on what you do with it. Organize big events that help your community and perhaps even a national audience. Maybe you like to sing or dance, ever think about using your talents in a unique way to help others? There are dozens of global mission trips that serve numerous functions – perhaps helping in a health care clinic in an impoverished village; or working in a vision camp to help the visually impaired. Interested in technology and making a small but meaningful change? Perhaps a mobile application might be an interesting and unique venture.

There's no shortage of ways to go above and beyond and no "right answer." Most of all, if you're activity can answer the question: "Am I serving those that are less fortunate in a meaningful way?" then you are on your way to success. Try different things and find what you love. Sometimes your passion for things isn't found until you experiment.

Planning Ahead: A Sample Timeline

To be a competitive BS/MD applicant you should start planning by the summer before ninth grade. From this date, your school year and summer activities are divided. Below is a suggested timeline in order for you to get all the experiences you need to have a strong application, prepare yourself for the interview, and, more importantly, for medical school. Don't worry about doing these in this exact order. There is a lot of flexibility here and not doing one or two of these things based on the timeline below will not prevent you from being successful. This is not a prescription or magic formula; rather these are suggestions to help you accomplish everything in order to have the strongest application possible.

Summer before 9th grade begins: *Create your timeline and map it out. Volunteer at a local hospital. Look for shadowing opportunities. Plan to take 1 AP/IB course if offered during the school year.*

9th grade school year: *Volunteer, take an AP/IB course, begin looking for summer research opportunities or school research programs. Participate in different clubs/sports and be active in them.*

Summer before 10th grade: *Volunteer, shadow & begin research. Take an SATII if you have taken a relevant AP/IB course (i.e. SAT in Biology after AP Biology).*

10th grade school year: *Volunteer, enroll for AP/IB courses; take an AP/IB exam and relevant SATII exam. Look for shadowing opportunities. Continue to be active in clubs/sports and seek out leadership opportunities within them. Continue to build relationships with teachers for future recommendation letters. Look for summer research programs and apply early!*

Summer before 11th grade: *Volunteer & Shadow. Begin or continue* *research. Study for SAT (1st sitting should be sometime in Junior Year). Take SATII for any relevant AP/IB courses.*

11th grade school year: *Continue volunteering & shadowing. Enroll in AP/IB courses and take AP/IB exams along with relevant SATII exams. 1st SAT sitting should be between the middle and end of Junior year. Strive to get a couple leadership positions under your belt by this year. Look for and apply to summer research programs. Build relationships with teachers.*

Summer before 12th grade: *Keep accumulating volunteer & shadowing hours, as well as research experiences. College application process begins: Start researching BS/MD programs and compile a list of potential programs based on your specific SAT/GPA criteria. Start writing your essays based on what each program requests, the most common being: "Why Medicine?" Study for and take SAT exam again if necessary.*

12th grade school year: *Take SAT exam if needed. Continue volunteering/shadowing on weekends. Continue involvement with clubs/sports. Finish application process and begin/complete interview process. Study for AP/IB exams for the end of the year (many colleges take AP/IB credit - so scoring well will help you in the long run - don't let 'Senioritis' hit too hard!). Apply for scholarships and submit your acceptance to the college program of your dreams. Prepare for and complete interviews, and then wait for hopeful acceptances!*

Summer before college: *Explore the world! Enjoy & Have fun!*

*If you haven't started the summer before 9th grade, don't worry. This is the ideal timeline. The earlier you begin doing these though, the better. At the absolute latest you should start volunteering by the 11th grade in order to accumulate enough hours and experience.

The Application

Your application to a combined medical program includes your SAT/ACT scores, high school transcript, résumé, CommonApp essays, supplementary essays, and recommendation letters. Some schools operate strictly through the CommonApp system, but others require supplementary applications to be filled out from their BS/MD program information website. The website of the specific BS/MD program will be your ultimate resource as to how you will need to submit your application. *Be meticulous and organized and make sure you don't miss any piece of the application*! For any further questions or for clarifications, contact the program admissions office directly via phone or email.

When preparing to start your application:

1. Look through the list of programs and see which could be of interest to you. Certainly look at all the programs in the state where you live. Many program favor in-state applicants over out-of-state applicants. Some programs are only for residents of that state.

2. Based on where you stand in comparison to the various criteria (SAT/GPA/ACT, rank, etc) apply to as many programs as you can in order to maximize your possibility for acceptance. For example, if you are just about average in terms of qualifications, you might need to apply to around fifteen programs with a mix of "reach," "match," and "safety." If you are in the top one-quarter, you may only need to apply to around ten or so. Of course there are financial considerations to applying to many programs as well, so take this

into account. To some extent, the more interviews you receive (and are prepared well for), the higher your chances of success.

3. Be sure to have schools that fall under each of these categories: Safety, Match, and Reach. While the terms are self-explanatory, here is some explanation anyway. "Safety" are schools in which your application is more competitive than the average and which will likely invite you for an interview. "Match" are schools where your application fits within the average and where you still have a good chance of being interviewed. "Reach" are schools where your application falls under the average, and getting an interview would be a "Woo Hoo!" moment. Above these, you should also apply to regular undergraduate programs as a backup in case you don't gain admission into a BS/MD program. When choosing which regular colleges you will be applying to, many factors must be weighed, but it all depends on you. Some people who do not gain admission into a BS/MD program may want to attend a competitive IVY league school. Others may want to attend a college that has a strong pre-med program while paying a low tuition for the first four years. Apply to places you may actually consider attending. So if you're not planning to attend Harvard even if you gain acceptance, there's no point in applying. If you are unsure, go ahead and apply and you can make that decision later.

4. Thoroughly review all the information on each program. Go through all of their online material—both on the undergraduate college and on the medical school. Remember, in an interview, you will be asked why you want to go to their program in particular. Remember, too, that you are expected to attend both the college and the medical school. Some programs (termed: non-binding) allow you to take the MCAT and apply for medical school via the traditional route if you wanted to attend a medical school not

affiliated with your specific program. Other programs (termed: binding) do not allow you to apply out to a different medical school and you must attend the medical school affiliated with your program. These are facts you want to know well before walking in to an interview.

5. Remember that everything on the application counts. That is, you may be average in your test scores, but if you have some research experience, or exceptional volunteer or shadowing experience that you talk about in your essays eloquently, you will be looked upon favorably.

6. Have a checklist for each BS/MD program you plan to apply to, and pay special attention to all the deadlines, which are typically earlier than regular college admission – the earliest being November 1st. Create this checklist in advance (during the summer before senior year) to give yourself ample time to meet these requirements if necessary. Some of the things applicants forget to do and run out of time for include: requesting additional recommendation letters; meeting the minimum number of volunteer hours; and taking the SATII for a specific subject test. One of the most important details of planning ahead is to know when you need to send in your application. Be sure you know this deadline and have everything ready for it.

Your application will be the paper version of who you are. In other words, it will tell the reader everything about you – from what you have done to what others think about you. With that being said, make sure that the different components of your application say something unique and different about you, if possible. One common mistake students make is in the essay. Do NOT write your main CommonApp essay or Personal Statement answering the question "Why do you want to be a doctor" unless the program does not ask that question in the supplementary questions. My personal strategy is I used the "Why Medicine" essay as my personal statement in the main CommonApp only if the school did not ask for that question anywhere else. If they did ask it in the supplementary section, I had another essay ready to submit to them as my personal statement. I definitely understand that this may be a tad time-consuming, but it is worth it. The reason is because the majority of supplementary essays will ask you the "Why Medicine" question anyway, asking you to describe your motivation to pursue a career in medicine. You do not want to answer the question two times for them (once through the CommonApp and again through the supplementary essay) because then you've lost an opportunity to speak to them about another important part of your character. I wrote my main CommonApp essay on one characteristic about myself, and used my activity (i.e. research) as an example. While you may not feel that this is true right now, the more essays a school requires, the better. You get to show them different parts of your personality. So use it effectively.

It is needless to say but important to say nonetheless: make sure to have someone proofread your application, résumé and essay. Nothing is more embarrassing than simple typos or grammatical errors.

* * * * *

The Résumé

Your résumé is a summary of your qualifications and experience. It should be no more than two pages. With only a glance, it should communicate the essence of your qualifications to be admitted to the BS/MD program. In it, you should describe important activities in a sentence or so and do not elaborate too much. If you've done research, list a couple bullet points on what you did research on and what techniques you may have used/learned. If you've had a research publication, list it. You'll want to include and focus especially on leadership opportunities you've had. It is often cited that committee members spend less than 60 seconds on the résumé, so make sure it is as clear and easy-to-read as possible.

Your résumé should be professional in nature. It should not have fancy colors or any pictures. You'll notice many résumés have somewhat advanced layouts and formatting – but ensure that no template you use is overtly distracting. Using a template is absolutely the best way to go when it comes time to creating a résumé. Simply listing your experiences in a MS Word document will not be enough. See the appendix for two samples containing the types of headers and details to include, as well as how to include them stylistically. I also include a free video on the website detailing this.

Make sure to catalogue and frequently update your résumé throughout the year with all the activities you are involved in. You do not want to forget any of your experiences nor do you want to spend half a day filling in your résumé, only to forget some key aspects.

Note: If a program asks for your curriculum vitae (CV), don't be alarmed. A CV is essentially the same thing, except it is typically more detailed. Consider it a more specific résumé.

FAQS:

Can a résumé include SAT/ACT/SATII scores?
- Sure, colleges will see the results anyway when you send them the official report so it is not necessary. But feel free to put it if it is really good and stands out!

Can I list total hours volunteered instead of weekly commitment?
- No problem, some programs or the CommonApp may ask you later how many hours per week you have volunteered so be prepared for that.

I have no employment history, is that OK?
- It's not a problem. Having employment is probably the least important component of your resume, but it adds a little bit of value since it shows more real-world experience. But don't fret if you don't have a job. Everything else is way more important.

I have no publications for my research yet. Can I state that I wrote a paper on it?
- It's best to include it if you have published or are submitting for publication. But if you have written an extensive paper on the culmination of your research and submitted it to various competitions or presented your paper somewhere, by all means, include this!

Should I include a description of all my activities?
- Don't include a full, lengthy description. Add a sentence or two to describe what you did in your experience. You want to keep your resume short (2 pages), and adding lengthy descriptions won't facilitate that. Remember, a CV is more detailed than a résumé.

The "Why Medicine" Essay

The "Why do you want to be a physician" essay you include as part of your application is considered as important as your qualifying academic achievement. In other words, it is a critical component, one that requires your fullest attention.

There are four areas you have to cover in your essay. Each must clearly communicate who you are so that the BS/MD application review committee can get a feel for you as a person and understand your motivation for not only becoming a physician but for applying to their school.

1. Why do you want to be a medical doctor? What in your life has made you want to become a doctor? Who impacted you? Which experiences?

2. How have you demonstrated your seriousness and commitment for the field of medicine? School? Work? Volunteer? Research?

3. Why are you interested in this particular BS/MD program? Do you understand its focus, its uniqueness, and its expectations? What do you know about its faculty, its student body, and its clinical or research opportunities?

4. Are you mature enough to make it through the program? This isn't a question you necessarily answer directly, but the quality of your response to the three other principal questions, and how you speak about your life, and life choices, and understanding as related to medicine will reflect your overall maturity and empathy and allow the review board to understand you as a person.

Much of the content of your essay will be addressed in your personal interview. In your essay you are not trying to put on a face that isn't you. Rather, your goal is simply to express yourself clearly as you are. Your ultimate goal is to leave the program's review committee with an unambiguous picture of you as a serious candidate that they want to meet in person.

How to write the "Why Medicine" essay

The most important thing in the essay is to convey why you want to become a physician. What in your life sparked or piqued your interest? The best essays often tell a very descriptive story. (Bear in mind you have to maintain a 2-page limit for most programs).

Some people have started off their essay describing a scene in the emergency room while they were volunteering. Others have talked about more personal experiences with the field. The ultimate goal is to tell a story by painting a picture. You can imagine that these colleges see thousands of the same applications (I wanted to be a doctor ever since I was a little kid, etc.). By the way, please don't use this one, as it is the most cliché line. Making it a more unique essay with vivid descriptions will distinguish your essay from the rest.

For the sake of having a unique essay, look at a few samples. Doing so gives you more ideas about structure, possible approaches and prevents you from creating just a duplicate of some other essay. Here are a couple sites with essays. Again, do not duplicate any of these essays. Instead, describe the main reason, a story if you will, on how you became first interested in the field. Paint a picture!

http://www.stars21.com/freemorn/ads/essay/medical_school_essa y_sample.html
http://www.medfools.com/personalstatements/premed/med-school-statement.php

With these guidelines, brainstorm ideas or events in your head and begin writing. Take the introductory paragraph slow. Make sure it has a hook - something to grab the reader and draw him/her in. This is usually the most vibrant scene in your essay. Don't rush your thoughts and don't rush the essay. In the final paragraph, make sure to end with a holistic idea or thought you derived as to why you want to pursue a career in medicine.

The biggest mistake students make is simply describing each part of their resume and talking about how it enhanced their desire to become a doctor. Don't do this! Do not simply talk about how volunteering helped, then how research helped, then how school helped, etc. While you can mention some of these things in the essay, focus on one or two unique ideas. Give concrete reasoning as to why you want to become a physician, and use examples from your experiences to supplement this.

Ask your friends, family, teachers and mentors to read your essay. Get their feedback about whether you are really expressing your personality through your words. When you feel you have said everything, make sure to have someone else edit it for spelling errors, grammar and style. Your English teacher may be a good person to ask.

The Interview

When you get your notification that the admissions committee wants to interview you, celebrate! They like everything (or mostly everything) the see on your application, and want to make sure you are going to be a good match for their program based on your personality (interview). So getting an interview is a huge deal, and you should be proud to make it this far! You now know that your application was good enough for the program to be interested in you. You've made the first and most difficult cut.

There are many ways to prepare for an interview, but if you wrote your essay properly, you have already accomplished the most important preparation: you have told them who you are, honestly—and they like it. The interview is simply about two things: 1) they would like to admit you to their program, so as part of their job they need to meet you in person to verify you are who you painted yourself as and 2) they want to see what you know about their program and what it would mean to you to be in it. They have to do this to assure themselves that you will be able to see it through and are excited to be there. This is especially true for out-of-state students. The interview is the time to convey your personality in a way that paper cannot. Be genuine, be kind, be empathetic and smile!

What will the interview be like? They can vary between programs. You will likely have a one-on-one interview with at least one member of an admissions committee and/or a panel interview and/or multiple-mini interviews (MMI). You will usually go to the school on a set day, tour the school and have a chance to ask questions, and do interviews. You will be expected to dress appropriately for an interview: suit and tie for males, professional dress clothes for females. However you dress, you should feel relaxed and comfortable. How you dress should reflect your respect for the college and the medical profession. It should also show your seriousness. At the same time, how you dress should just as easily go un-noticed. You want to be a physician, not a fashion designer. No jeans and t-shirts, and go easy on the piercings!

You will be expected to discuss the things that you put on your essays about why you want to go to that school and why you wish to become a physician. Depending on the school, you may be asked about your high school activities, volunteering, research and any shadowing you have done. While you should bring a copy of your résumé, don't use it for reference during the interview. Remember that you may be asked about anything you put on your application so make sure you know it inside and out.

In general, admissions committee members who interview high school students for medical school programs are experienced at these interviews and recognize the differences between high school and college students. You will not be expected to have the number and type of standard pre-med experiences that would have been typical for college students. You will be more likely asked somewhat general questions about your interest in science, the types of things you like to read, and about your non-scientific activities in school. Make sure to tell the whole truth about yourself and your background. Some programs may ask you questions about ethics in healthcare. They may also ask you about current healthcare policies and areas for reform so it is important to research this information and stay up-to-date in the field.

Remember when we talked earlier about applying to many programs? Well, don't be surprised if you hear back from many of them. If you're invited to interview at more than 10, discuss with a counselor or an advisor because you may not (and probably shouldn't) go traveling cross-country to interview at each and every program. Let alone, you're still enrolled in high school and probably can't be absent for weeks on end. Again, this is an individualistic financial and time consideration.

How to prepare for the interview

As with any other applicant, admissions committee members are looking for your maturity, your empathy, your ability to communicate ideas thoroughly and amicably, your passion to pursue medicine, and for evidence that you are likely be committed to the program. Most admission committee members believe that at the age of 16 or 17, high school students cannot know how they want to spend the rest of their lives—and maybe this is true for some applicants—but your job in the interview is to demonstrate how you are the exception.

Think about the following questions. How would you answer them? What kinds of examples, or supporting evidence, would you include? They want to see eloquence in your communication but definitely not rehearsed eloquence because that often comes across as fake. Be natural and genuine.

These are some of the generic questions you will receive:

Tell me about yourself.

When did you first decide you wanted to go to medical school?

Why do you want to pursue a career in medicine?

If you had a second choice for a career, what would it be and why?

What about a combined degree program especially appeals to you?

What are your favorite books (or most recently read non-school book) and why?

Who has talked with you about medical school and what did you learn from them about it?

Who has been most significant influence in your decision to become a doctor?

What has been your greatest challenge thus far and how have you dealt with it?

What has volunteering taught you? What was the most difficult experience you had in volunteering? The most rewarding?

What are your greatest strengths/weaknesses?

Who is your role model and why?

Behavioral questions are becoming more commonplace in interviews. The goal is to assess how you have handled certain difficult or 'sticky' situations in the past. There are a few extremely common examples of behavioral questions that we will go over in this section. These are used frequently in all kinds of interviews, not limited to BSMD, medical school, even job interviews. The purpose of behavioral questions is to extrapolate from an interviewees answer how they might deal with similar situations in the future. Therefore, they tend to be common scenarios that you have undoubtedly come across in many different settings in your past experiences. Below are a few very common behavioral questions:

Describe a time when you worked in a team

Describe a time you overcame adversity/how do you deal with conflict?

Describe a time when you acted as a leader

Describe a time when you disagreed with someone and had to vocalize your concerns

Describe a time when you were upset with the behavior of someone in your team and how you overcame it

Describe a time when you tried to accomplish something and failed

Tell me about a time your performance was criticized

Describe a time when you made a mistake and had to tell someone

Tell me about a time you were disappointed in your performance

Tell me about a time you worked under pressure/stressful situation

Tell me about a pet peeve you have.

To answer these kinds of questions, you should use the STAR format. STAR stands for situation, task, action, and result.

Situation: Spend 1-2 sentences providing a proper background for your answer. Give the interviewer details about the scenario so that they can picture it for themselves.

Task: This is when you bring in the specific behavioral question they are asking. Why were you required to work as a team? What was the adversity that presented itself? Why were you acting as leader?

This is where you would introduce the "dilemma" that you will be solving.

Action: You would then delve into what YOU did in this situation. What were your concerns? What was the purpose behind your action?

Result: Finally, explain what came of the situation based on your action

You may be thinking, how could I possibly prepare for behavioral questions if I don't know which one they are going to ask? The trick is, examples, examples, examples. Always have 5-10 stories in your back pocket that can be applied to different scenarios. This takes creativity and introspection. Look back on ALL of your previous experiences and try to pull examples from your schoolwork, research, personal life, extracurricular activity, leadership positions, etc, so that no matter the question, you have some form of a strong example to lend support to your argument. It's not uncommon that these examples can help you not only on behavioral and situational questions, but on really any interview question you could possibly be asked.

Situational questions are another group of questions you can be asked. The main difference between these questions and a behavioral question is that the situational question puts you in a hypothetical environment while a behavioral question asks you to reflect on an event that has already happened. The primary goal of a situational question will be to assess your problem solving skills. You might be asked to imagine a hypothetical environment where there are two difficult possible routes to take as a course of action. Your job is to imagine the setting, process the possible solutions, and to articulate which solution takes priority over the other and for what reasons. These types of questions will largely assess your ability to problem solve, triage (or prioritize more urgent tasks over less urgent ones), and handle interpersonal conflicts professionally. These questions allow an interview to see how you think through a problem, how you react to adversity, and how you articulate a well composed answer. You'll be able to use this time to demonstrate your professionalism, problem solving skills, and compassion.

It is impossible to practice every situational question (as you can imagine) but here are some examples:

Let's say you are in clinic and are seeing a patient. Your nurse knocks on your door and says there is a patient who is not on the schedule who urgently asked to see you right away. What do you do?

You're working on a project with a tight deadline and have delegated tasks to various team members. The day before the deadline, a few of your team members have not contributed their fare share of work. What do you do?

Some of the more competitive programs may present ethical questions related to current issues in medicine or health care policy. Most of the time there is no right or wrong to these questions, but they are helpful to the admissions committee to see how much you have thought about medicine and how you approach such difficult and/or complex issues. When answering these questions, the most important aspect of your answer is that you justify your position well. Examples of such questions are as follows:

What do you think the doctor's role is in abortion?

When do you think life begins?

What is your opinion on stem cell research?

What role does nutrition play in preventive medicine?

What is the biggest problem in healthcare now and how can it be addressed in the next five years?

What do you think about Medicaid? Medicare?

When do you think euthanasia is appropriate?

It is important to stay abreast of all the different topics in healthcare (and for bonus points – outside of health care as well) so you can talk intelligently about them.

Ask your friends and teachers to help you come up with questions. Really think about them, discuss them. Write down your answers in a document/book so you can remember the points you want to be sure to convey by the end of the question (not for the sake of memorizing a script).

When you practice answering questions, practice making eye contact. Then practice it some more, and work on your speaking skills with someone who is willing to give you honest feedback. Oftentimes people ask about hiring an interview coach. It can be helpful for some but can also be expensive. We are working to provide resources on the website to enhance your interview preparation without spending an arm and leg.

Enjoy the interview. Be interested. Be interested in the questions.

Most importantly, smile—it goes a long way

*We have prepared an **extensive** video course series (titled: **Combined BS/MD Program Interview Mastery Training Series**) on our website at directbsmd.com under the Tab "Interview Course" (link: https://interviewmd.teachable.com/). This was created solely with the goal of enhancing your interview skills, so you will look your best on interview day. It is a one-hour long, extensive interview preparation series and goes over every nut and bolt of preparing for an interview. This resource will significantly supplement your interview preparation, and is particularly useful for those that want more guided help. We're excited for you to try it out!

The "Do Nots."

There are some things to avoid doing in an interview. Here's a list of some of them.

1. Do not indicate that you want to do one of these programs just so you can be sure of getting into medical school.

2. Do not speak informally to your interviewer. Be who you are, but remember this is a formal, professional interview. Avoid any slang expressions and be courteous.

3. Do not panic if you don't have an answer to a question. Just say, "I'm not really sure, but I'll think about it/look it up." If you feel you know the answer but may need a few seconds to think it through, then take those few seconds with silence rather than prefacing your answer with ten seconds of an "umm" or "uhh."

4. Although you will be nervous, have someone practice with you so you can become sensitive to your nervous habits such as twirling

your hair, fidgeting, tapping on the desk, scratching yourself, picking at your fingernails, biting your lip, looking down, and so on. Interviewers often are interested in seeing how you react under more stressful conditions, and any exaggerated nervous habit may create an unfavorable impression. This is likely one of your first interviews so feedback on your interview is particularly crucial at this stage.

5. Do not insult any school. Never say that you went into this program because other programs are not as good. You interviewer will rightly think that you will speak badly of them in your interviews at other schools.

6. Do not spend excessive time or energy working on your appearance. Look nice, but be yourself. You want to come across as neat and polished. More on this below.

7. Do not waste time apologizing for or explaining one bad grade or your first SAT score that wasn't as good as you would have liked. If an interviewer addresses it, give a concise and truthful answer, but do not let it take away from the rest of the interview. In fact, you may be able to turn it into a positive by discussing how you were able to improve and grow from that experience. If you are interviewing for a program, they already assume you are smart enough to succeed.

What makes a strong interview?

Above all, the admissions committee is looking for your passion for medicine, for your maturity and empathy. They know you are about seventeen or eighteen years old, but even at that age, they believe they can learn something from what you say and how you say it.

Tell them your story—what makes you unique? Why will you enjoy going into medicine? If you have done music or sports, tell them how committed you can be to what you do. They'll understand that you can transfer this commitment to your medical studies. If you've traveled somewhere unique or done anything special, describe it and be enthusiastic, but not boastful, about it. Interviewees most often note that it is hard to not sound like they are boasting when they are trying to explain what makes them a great applicant. A great approach often is to demonstrate how others helped you achieve your goals; this demonstrates teamwork, deference and humility – admirable traits to have as a physician. It is a hard line, but practice and feedback are essential here!

Next steps:

Finally, the interviews are rolling in! You selected your dates, booked your flights, got all your ducks in a row. Only a few days left, and one subtle but BIG problem sets in your mind..."what do I wear?" Believe it or not, how you dress for an interview is one of many important components to your whole package. As an aspiring physician, it's essential to come off as a bright and engaging student, but also as a person who is well put-together.

Quick Tips:

1. Always choose professional colors: navy blue, white, black, beige and grey are the go-to options and need to make up the most of your outfit.

2. Choose clothes that fit well. Half the battle is finding an outfit that fits your body frame, but this is the key to making any outfit look sharp. The fashion side of me wants to convey to you that, when you take finances into consideration, a well-tailored suit is more important than a high quality suit. Nonetheless, you'll want a suit that can withstand the wear and tear of traveling.

3. When it comes to patterns like argyle, stripes, and plaid, subtlety is key. First off, no two patterns should be used together, and

second, ANY pattern that is used should blend well with the overall outfit rather than stand out like a sore thumb. When in doubt, solids are always the way to go!

4. Stay professional. Looking sharp is more important than having an extremely stylish and unique outfit.

The below section was written by a fellow guest BS/MD graduate:

LADIES: Often, this is the hardest part of preparing for the interview, with every other website or resource or older sibling saying to wear something different. For the record, pant suits, skirt suits, and professional dresses are ALL acceptable. However, choosing a dress requires a careful selection for something both modest and professional. That being said, modesty is an important component to any outfit, so be sure to choose skirts or dresses that come to the knee even when seated. Also as a general rule of thumb, necklines should not come lower than one or two inches below the collarbone. And lastly the topic everyone dreads...shoes. For the record once again, flats and high heels are both acceptable. But in this case, ladies need to be as practical as possible. Most interview days include a tour of hospital facilities, undergraduate campuses, and sometimes dorms – shoes NEED to be comfortable.

GENTLEMEN: Guys, not too much extra to consider, luckily! A sharp suit is your best accessory. Remember to learn to tie a tie well before the night prior to your interview (or ensure that your dad is on hand). And when it comes to shoes, dress shoes are a must!

Pack your iron and lint rollers, and be sure to prepare your outfit the night before the interview! **Look sharp, and good luck!**

*After you've started to gain acceptances into programs, review the earlier chapter titled: "Which Program Should I Choose?" to help you make an informed decision.

Check out DirectBSMD.com under the tab "Interview Course" or visit interviewmd.teachable.com for an extensive interview preparation series.

Alternative Professional Medical Programs (Naturopathy, Chiropractic, Osteopathy, Homeopathy, Oriental Medicine, Acupuncture, Overseas training)

Becoming a medically trained doctor (M.D.) is a particular approach to medicine and healing. It is based in the western philosophical tradition, with strong reliance on the scientifically and materialistically based experimental approach. There are alternatives both within this approach and different from this approach. Some admissions interviewers may want to see if you know that there are such alternatives and if you have considered them as alternatives to traditional medical school. They might ask this as another means to explore the foundations of your commitment to western medicine, and/or to see if you have a fall-back plan in case you are not accepted into a BS/MD program.

Professional alternatives generally based on the western philosophical/materialist paradigm:
   ◆   Ph.D. in medically related sciences such as physiology, anatomy, biochemistry, pharmacy, and so forth
   ◆ Physician's Assistant (PA) or Nurse Practitioner (NP)
   ◆ Nursing
   ◆ Medical or laboratory technologist
   ◆ Medical research not requiring either a PhD. or a M.D.
   ◆ Naturopathy
   ◆ Chiropractic
   ◆ Osteopathy (In the United States a Doctor of Osteopathy has the same status and rights as a M.D.). Discussion of D.O. degree below.

♦ An alternative to attending a medical school in the United States is to earn an M.D. overseas. Most countries admit foreign students.

♦ Veterinary Medicine.

Professional alternatives not based in the western philosophical scientific/materialist paradigm:

♦ Doctor of Oriental Medicine.
♦ Licensed Acupuncturist or Doctor of Acupuncture.
♦ Doctor of Homeopathy.
♦ Doctor of Ayurvedic Medicine.

* * * * *

D.O. PROGRAMS

There's more than one way to fulfill your lifelong passion of becoming a doctor. Here's another one. BS/DO programs have arisen as an alternative form of BS/MD programs.

Direct BS/DO programs offer a combined Baccalaureate (B.S.)/doctor of osteopathic (D.O) degrees right out of high school! Similar in structure to a BS/MD program, but with a D.O. degree.

Traditionally these programs can be completed in 7 or 8 years straight out of high school. This program guarantees a student's admission into a medical school after completing the program's undergraduate requirements. After graduating from the medical school, the student graduates with a D.O. degree (Doctor of Osteopathic Medicine) degree and is able to practice a career in medicine.

Combined BS/DO programs are slightly less competitive than BS/MD programs and for those programs that require the MCAT to be taken, the MCAT requirement is often lower.

While the differences between an M.D. and D.O. degree are scarce, there are some aspects of both degrees that are worth mentioning. D.O.s generally focus on the patient as a whole and focus on preventative care. It is a field of medicine called osteopathic medicine. Generally speaking, or at least historically speak, the focus of the D.O. is to use one's hands to diagnose illnesses and avoid using medicine as the solution. Instead, they encourage the body to heal itself. D.O.s usually receive extra training in the musculoskeletal system.

However, D.O.s and M.D.s both take the same medical school admission exam, the MCAT, and spend four years studying medicine. Through a 3-7 year residency program, both the MD and the D.O. are able to specialize in an area of medicine. Some D.O.s complete the same residency programs as MDs. D.O.s usually take the COMLEX to get in to osteopathic residencies and MDs take the USMLE to get into medical residencies. However, D.O.s looking to get a medical residency must take the USMLEs as well. Some residency programs are restricted to MDs, and some osteopathic residency programs are restricted to D.O.s.

All in all, D.O.s perform the same job as M.D.s these days. There is little to no discrepancy except in the actual degree conferred. D.O.s may be slightly limited by the type of residencies they may be able to get into later on. I found out recently that the doctor that had delivered me as a baby was actually a D.O. The medical community, once you have a job, does not look down upon the D.O. degree as some may claim. As a D.O. you have the same job description as an M.D. – to heal the sick and ease suffering.

* * * * *

Unique Advice from Other BS/MD Students

I was able to recruit some colleagues who wanted to give their thoughts about the BS/MD process; information that could be very useful to hear. I thought it would beneficial for readers to have perspectives from several other people. The first question I asked them was: *What is one piece of advice you wish you had known before beginning the combined BS/MD program applications?* The second question was: *What is one part of your specific application you feel helped the most to gain admission into a BS/MD program?* And then I offered them a chance to contribute any additional comments they might have. So here are some BS/MD student profiles!

Student #1

What is one piece of advice you wish you had known before beginning the combined BS/MD program applications?

"There's actually a lot I wished I knew before applying or even interviewing for these Combined Med Programs. If I had known earlier, I would have expanded my parameters for research even more, maybe find a spot in a lab, continue to compete further in upper-tier national science fair competitions, like Intel. But on a more local perspective, I wish I could have explored a variety of shadowing opportunities. The one piece of advice that I wish I had was: don't be afraid to go that extra step, to explore, to ask, and to be competitive by searching for your own unique experiences that could help you stand out as an applicant. During the interview, I remember seeing students bringing research posters with such high level content and conversing with kids who weren't afraid to go to hospitals and ask doctors in many different departments, like cardiology and pediatrics, if they could obtain a position shadowing physicians they may have never known before. So basically, I wish I knew that I should have gone the extra mile to create much more meaningful experiences and taken more effort in finding opportunities that would have made me a more outstanding applicant. Don't be afraid to do that!"

What is one part of your specific application you feel helped the most to gain admission into a BS/MD program?

"Although my resume wasn't what people would think of as the 'ultimate resume for a competitive med school student,' the small experiences I did have were very meaningful and pertinent to my future career as a physician. My essays were also written articulately to reflect the major lessons I've learned from these experiences and analyzed how these lessons are significant for a future doctor. For example, like many other applicants I'm sure, I volunteered at my local hospital. But it didn't just involve filing and giving out water and food for patients (not to undermine this role in any way—each job has its own significance). My role as a Friendly Visitor further developed into my realization of the interaction between a doctor and patient, since the job involved communicating and establishing effective relationships with patients, dealing with their emotional dilemmas, understanding their experiences and mindset, and then carefully crafting your own dialogues to avoid sensitive topics like politics, family life, a loss, or their conditions. So mastering the bedside manner was a major skill obtained in this job. Even small jobs and services like this was advantageous for my application since I was able to analyze and be enthusiastic about it in my essays and interviews. Although admissions officers aren't able to physically see you when deciding the status of your application, they are able to sense your personality and whether or not you are genuinely enthusiastic about this profession. I believe my essays did reflect how passionate and committed I am to my service and genuinely involved I am in my work, and it did so while eliminating any generic content saying "how I want to help out in the future" as the reason for becoming a doctor. I would also have to say also that of my experiences, some unique opportunities I thankfully had before applying for these programs may have held the interest of my admissions officers as well. This includes a medical conference that I attended during high school where I experienced the life of a medical student in a week (including viewing cadavers, visiting the hospitals, learning how to properly conduct a physical, attending lectures led by renown medical doctors and professors, discussing controversial and ethical dilemmas in medicine today, and understanding how to deal with the diversity and the cultural/religious perspectives of patients that may interfere with medical practices). So again if you are offered these kinds of opportunities, don't be afraid to go for it because it can leave an impression on admissions officers. Along with these experiences, the numbers do matter after all. Being in the higher end of the spectrum when it comes to grades and SAT/ACT scores does undeniably have its advantages. Meeting the minimum standards to get an interview may be a good thing, but I think that surpassing that standard helps everyone without a doubt!"

Additional comments:

"I know this may be repetitive, but I cannot emphasize this enough: don't be afraid to go that extra step to find and accept new and rare opportunities. Being an active student shows admissions that you will be a very involved and dedicated med school student capable of surpassing limitations. Looking in the retrospect, if I hadn't been afraid to do that, I may have built a stronger resume that could have been my ticket to a much more competitive program on the national scale, although I am very satisfied and thankful for getting into the program I currently am in. But seriously, don't worry about not knowing the physician or having to go out of your way to explore hospitals or research facilities on your own. The fact that you are so young and are still determined to seek such opportunities would gain you applause and appreciation from the admissions officers. So good luck and work hard to build a meaningful resume now to get into the program of your choice later!"

Student #2

What is one piece of advice you wish you had known before beginning the combined BS/MD program applications?

"SATs are a big make it or break it. Some schools only look at these for a cutoff. So even when I had a great GPA, and great extracurriculars, some schools only considered students with top SAT scores since the programs are so competitive. So it is so important to spend time preparing for the SATs and to do your best cause it will definitely affect the admission process. "

What is one part of your specific application you feel helped the most to gain admission into a BS/MD program?

"I think for the programs I applied to really valued my years of volunteering. It was so important because it showed so many aspects of myself-that I like to help others, that I wanted to be a doctor after I had seen what doctors have done, and the number of years showed a commitment. They don't want applicants who are committing to a career when they have no idea what the job entails. "

Additional comments:

"GPAs, SATs, and extracurriculars are so important for getting an interview. After getting an interview notification, make sure to practice for interviews!! Some schools really base their admission decision on the interview so it is important to have your best version shown. "

Student #3

What is one piece of advice you wish you had known before beginning the combined BS/MD program applications?

"I wish I had research experience. I think it would have increased the number of interviews I was invited to."

What is one part of your specific application you feel helped the most to gain admission into a BS/MD program?

"I had a huge amount of volunteer hours and a huge amount of shadowing hours. But I also had a lot of random other experiences to diversify my extracurriculars like Junior Statesmen of America and Invisible Children. Also I did some unique shadowing experiences outside of physicians, one with a midwife, and one with a medical malpractice lawyer that helped me see medicine from completely different perspectives, so when I went for interviews, I could say that I hadn't just seen it from a doctors perspective, I tried throughout high school to see all aspects of the career. "

Additional comments:

"Pass your AP tests because it makes you look like a serious student, whether they are relevant subjects or not. And admit to your mistakes but have a genuine reason why you made them during your interview. Be ready to be asked why you got a B (if relevant) here or why you didn't pass this test, or why you dropped out of that class because its likely to come up in some way or another at some interview."

Student #4

What is one piece of advice you wish you had known before beginning the combined BS/MD program applications?

"I had a lot of experience working in a clinic and volunteering at a hospital, but I had almost no research experience. Although it is not necessarily critical to have research experience, I think it would have made me a more well-rounded applicant and I would have been more prepared for being a part of a medical program in general. In my years as an undergraduate I know I have learned a lot from my research experiences and getting involved in research during high school would have been helpful."

What is one part of your specific application you feel helped the most to gain admission into a BS/MD program?

"I believe what helped me the most was the quality of my healthcare hours, not the quantity. I had about 400 volunteer hours, but I know several applicants that had more hours than I did. I had an internship in a clinic, in which I was able to see patients, take their medical history, check their vitals, draw blood for testing, and administer shots (under supervision of course). Direct patient contact is really important. Discharging patients at the hospital is good experience, but doing something that involves having a greater connection with patients is more valuable for a medical program application."

Additional comments:

"I think volunteering in a small clinic can be more beneficial than volunteering somewhere that has a large volume of volunteers, because it can help you get more individual attention. I was the only student volunteer at the small clinic where I worked, so I learned directly from the professional staff and I had the opportunity to do a little bit of everything."

Student #5

What is one piece of advice you wish you had known before beginning the combined BS/MD program applications?

"I wish I had known the extent to which some Combined Med Programs affiliated with public medical schools seemed to prefer in-state students. As an example, the NEOMED program interviews and accepts students mostly from the state of Ohio. Therefore, students should apply to all of the programs in their respective geographical locations. Private schools do not seem to place much emphasis on the geographical location of applicants."

What is one part of your specific application you feel helped the most to gain admission into a BS/MD program?

"I feel that having research experience helped me the most as it was one of the more 'unique' activities that high school students can partake in to kindle and thereafter demonstrate their passion in the field of medicine."

Additional comments:

"Prospective students should ensure that they can answer any questions regarding their applications. Some interviewers like to ask 'curveball' questions to see how the applicant reacts, and the best way to be prepared is to know what views you expressed in your application. Furthermore, students should be prepared to answer questions such as 'Why medicine?' and 'Why _____ School of Medicine/Program?'"

Student #6

What is one piece of advice you wish you had known before beginning the combined BS/MD program applications?

"I wish I had known how valuable 'research' was as an extracurricular activity/interest. As these programs become more competitive, applicants look more similar and become more difficult to distinguish. I feel that research is one of the few distinguishing characteristics. Researchers are wary to give positions to college students, so if a high school student can earn a spot on a research team, it shows deep interest and special aptitude. The act of doing research can expand academic horizons and earn acclaim that few applicants, if any, have."

What is one part of your specific application you feel helped the most to gain admission into a BS/MD program?

"I think my variety of healthcare experiences helped me the most. I shadowed a family physician, dentist, and physical therapist, and I also volunteered at my community hospital's volunteer workroom to transport patients and deliver lab specimens and meals. From all these experiences, I learned that healthcare was a rewarding, but challenging field. However, the variety showed me why medicine was right for me. As a physician, I would be involved from start to finish, from diagnosis to treatment. The other professions did not afford me that beautiful privilege."

Conclusion

If you have any questions about the application process or anything regarding the programs, I can do my best to help answer them! Email me at hello@directbsmd.com.

I hope your ride is smooth and hope that all the resources provided here in this book and the digital chart resource on the website will be of use to you. The website is being updated as often as I can given the time constraints of my training. If there are specific areas you would like to see my address in the next edition, please email me as well. This book is revised every year to provide you with not only the yearly reflections I obtain through my training, but also the specific advice you seek. I'd also encourage you to sign up for the newsletter where I try to impart any additional pearls that might be helpful for you. I'm truly excited and honored to help you achieve your dream of becoming a doctor. It is the most rewarding profession, and I humbled to be a part of it.

Thank you for reading, and for more up-to-date information, please visit: www.directbsmd.com

JOHN DOE

123 MAIN STREET • NEW YORK, NY 10065
Phone: (000) 555-5555 • E-Mail: first.last@mail.com

EDUCATION

Central High School, New York, New York   09/2010 – 06/2014
Cumulative Average: 104.5 *(weighted)*
  • 12 Advanced Placement (AP) Courses

RESEARCH EXPERIENCE

RESEARCH ASSISTANT
Institution of Research, City, State   12/2012 – Present
Mentor/PI: John Doe, Ph.D.
  • What did you do here?
  • List some specific things you have learned
  • Include any special techniques such as gel electrophoresis, etc.

RESEARCH SUMMER INTERN
Institution of Research, City, State   05/2010 – 08/2010
Mentor/PI: John Doe, M.D., Ph.D.
  • What did you do here?
  • List some specific things you have learned or done
  • Include any special techniques such as gel electrophoresis, etc.

PUBLICATIONS

Title of Paper: "The effect of hard work on academic success."
      Small description on the paper (if published or submitted for publishing)

HONORS & AWARDS

The Best Student Award   01/2011

National Honor Society   Grades 11, 12

Math Honor Society   Grades 11, 12

Foreign Language Honor Society   Grades 10, 11, 12

Advanced Placement (AP) Scholar with Distinction   Grades 10, 11, 12

Excellence in Spanish Award   Grades 9, 10, 11, 12

SHADOWING

DR. JOHN DOE
Hospital, City, State   10/2011 – Present
- What department? A few things you've learned from the experience.

DR. JANE DOE
Hospital, City, State   10/2011 – Present
- What department? A few things you've learned from the experience.

EXTRACURRICULAR ACTIVITIES

This club   Grades 9, 10, 11, 12
- My leadership position

That club   Grades 9, 10, 11, 12
- My leadership position

This club   Grades 9, 10, 11, 12
- My leadership position

This club   Grades 10, 11, 12

That organization   Grades 10, 11, 12

That involvement   09/2010

COMMUNITY SERVICE

Volunteer, Hospital, City, State   01/2011 – Present
(6 hours per week)

Volunteer, Hospital, City, State   01/2010 – 01/2011
(6 hours per week)

EMPLOYMENT HISTORY

JOB TITLE
Company, City, State   07/2011 – Present
- Write/list your job responsibilities

Sample Resume 2

John M. Dee

111 E. Medical Way
Madison, WI 99999
fmdee@email.com
Tel.: 111-222-3333

Goal: To practice the great science and art of medicine.

Academics, Jefferson High School, Madison, Wisconsin, 2009-2012
GPA 3.7
SAT 2100
SAT Math 690
SAT Science 720
SAT Chemistry 700
SAT Biology 760

Research
June – September 2011 Research assistant. *Relationship of L-dopa Therapy to Serotinin Depletion in the Psychiatric Patient,* Adam Crick, M.D., research director, University of Home State Medical School, Home State, USA

June – September 2012 Research associated *A Double Blind Comparative Study of Mutation Drivers Implied in the use of Penicillin Derivatives compared to Glycopeptide antibiotics on Hospital MRSA,* Richard Abley, M.D., research director, Charleston Immunological Research Institute, Charleston, Home State, USA.

Awards, Societies, and Projects
Honor Roll, 4 years.
Wisconsin Honor Society 20111, 2012
3rd place, State Science Award Competition, 2011

Medical experience
Volunteer: Position/service/function. Hospital/Institution Name. Unit. Supervisor name. One or two sentence description of what you did.

Shadow: Doctors name. Medical Specialty. Where shadowed. One or two sentence description of what you did.

Leadership
> Team Captain, varsity tennis, 2012
> Junior Class President, 2011
> Medical Club President, 2012

Extracurricular
> Varsity tennis, team captain 2012
> Medical Club 2010-2012
> High School Jazz band, 2010-2012

References

James Henry, counselor, Jefferson High School. jhenry@jeffersonhs.edu. Tel.: 111-123-2456
Robert Jackson, teacher, Jefferson High School. rjackson@jeffersonhs.edu. Tel.: 111-123-3322
Richard Abley, MD., research director, Charleston Immunological Research Institute.
r.abley@ciri.org. Tel 222-246-1357
Adam Crick, M.D., research director, University of Home State Medical School.
a.crick@hsms.org. Tel: 111-333-7676

My Program List   **Deadline**

1._____

2._____

3._____

4._____

5._____

6._____

7._____

8._____

9._____

10._____

11._____

12._____

13._____

14._____